Adriaan Bekman

The Horizontal Leadership Book

alertverlag.
bücher auf der höhe der zeit

Bibliografische Information der Deutschen Nationalbibliothek

Die Deutsche Nationalbibliothek verzeichnet diese Publikation in der Deutschen Nationalbibliografie; detaillierte bibliografische Daten sind im Internet über http://dnb.d-nb.de abrufbar

© Alert-Verlag, Berlin • www.alert-verlag.de
Rheinstraße 46, D–12161 Berlin, Tel. (0 30) 766 999-80

ISBN: 978-3-941136-07-6
1. Auflage 2010
Gestaltung: Michael Reichmuth, Berlin
Satz & Umbruch: Ulrich Bogun, www.satzservice.de
Sämtliche Rechte vorbehalten
Printed in Germany

Contents

Introduction

The Brazilian Carnival

Once I had the pleasure of visiting the carnival in Rio de Janeiro. A stand had been erected along a stretch of one and a half kilometers, and together with more than 80.000 Brazilians and visitors I saw samba schools filing past the stands in a boisterous and excited mood. I observed the spectacle with both compassion and admiration.

This procession was a perfect example of human organization. Following an unseen but precise master plan, enormous groups of beautifully dressed Brazilians were dancing the samba. Every samba school had its own theme, its own music, its own choreography, its own story to tell. It took one full hour for even one single school to pass by. First a group of dancing children approached, and then groups of older Brazilians, youngsters and a beautiful sexy couple. I saw gorgeously decked-out wagons, and there were men and women dancing on elevated platforms in an alluring and erotic fashion. The band played the same song during the whole time, and thereafter there was a break when a group of cleaners cleaned the street, swaying with their bodies to and fro.

Some Brazilian friends of mine, who had been dancing for many years in similar samba schools, explained how it is possible to organize an event like this in such a way: a samba school will be somewhere in the neighborhood. Anyone can join this school, either through family contacts or by paying an admission fee. A small group of people design the costumes and make sure that everything is in order. Every school organizes a competition for bands and then chooses a popular song for their show. All of the activities around the samba event are considered to be very "clean", as leadership is seldom in the hands of the local "Mafia". During the whole year people save up to buy their costumes. At first they study and practice the dance's choreography in small groups. Only on the night of performance itself does the whole act get put together. The schools participate in a competition and the winning samba school is invited to perform their show again the following night. Millions of people watch the great show on television.

This is a sublime example of the human capacity to organize. An enormous tourist business has gravitated towards this whole festival. Taxis, bars and restaurants have their best night of the year. If you think through all aspects of organizing an event of this magnitude like logistics, finances, people management, transport and so on, they are all present here, and it is a miracle that it all works in such a perfect way—even allowing for the natural Brazilian style and relaxed approach to all big things!

7

About this book

In this book, our image of organization and leadership is expressed very well by this little story of the Brazilian carnival. This miracle of human expression and organization is very much a result of what I in this book will call "horizontal leadership".

I will openly admit that this book is not about a new and successful management concept: you will not find cases of famous international companies from which you can learn and showing how to react in a similar situation; I will not show you wonderful success stories; I will not offer you the concepts you have to apply to be a successful leader. Therefore, I cannot offer you an impressive leadership development program.

However, this is a book about leadership. The content is based on the experiences and reflections of real-life people, who might be unknown to the general public, but who, nevertheless, are striving for the best. Their insights, which are being shared with you here, might inspire you to develop your own leadership style by researching and experimenting with the horizontal leadership methodology yourself.

To explore and demonstrate horizontal leadership in depth, I will use an unusual image of an organization. This image is about the organization as a living community, in which people individually create their personal biography and where they commonly create a company biography.

This book is about living, moving, organizational communities, which create sense in the individual's life of those participating in the process of its development.

Images of man and organization

To be able to do this, we will base our stories on an image of mankind, as it might be living in our souls. Our image of this man living in us guides us strongly in the way we treat ourselves and others in the social realm of working and private life. I will attempt to connect our images of the human being to the leadership issue, and I will also give some practical examples showing you how leaders deal with it. I will then also explore in more detail how today we see leaders develop and progress in their organizations, how they create change in them and take them through a transformation. In this mental journey I will touch upon the more fundamental views and ideas we have about organized society, which are directing us into an unknown future.

Being clearly outside of the usual area in which you might find a discussion on this subject, I will use a language in this book which is not the "usual" management jargon, but is what I will call the "horizontal leadership language". This language is used between people who are in a process of development together. It is a language we use when we jointly embark on exploring new realities, moving in uncharted waters. It is then about words and concepts like "paying attention", "having trust", "making the connection", "acting with love", "creating freedom", "taking responsibility", "showing respect", "caring for", "wrestling with", "deepening together", "making sense", "giving meaning", "crossing the threshold".

Overview

What is the basic design underlying this book's content, and how is this content structured in the different parts and chapters of this book?

The book consists of two parts.

Part one
Horizontal organizing . . . . Methods and tools
Horizontal leadership . . . . Making change happen

This part is the more conceptual and practical part, in which the basic thinking and our approach of the theme are described.

Part two
The leadership research methodology . . . . The basic thinking, the key ideas

This part is the more philosophical and methodological part, in which our unique and new contribution in these two areas is described and placed into the scientific context.

The nine chapters

Reading through the chapters and digesting the content leads to a better understanding of how horizontal leadership, organizing and Sense-Making are connected to each other. Today we live and work in complex realities, in which it can be seen as essential that we gain a new and better understanding of the Sense-Making process related to organizational development activities. Facing these activities, you stand and move as being a fundamental part of a leadership process in your organization yourself, in which the whole working community participates.

The buildup in chapters across the two parts follows a certain path of reasoning:

In chapter one, we are introduced to the traditional organizations as living communities in which people meet their destiny. We are confronted in organizations with the basic principles of creating organized communities that form a different kind of community than the natural communities we are born in. The organization is a living open organism, a developing community.

In chapter two, I will expand from this insight to see the organization as a living organism. This organism is supported by two dimensions—the vertical and the horizontal dimension—which are basically the dimensions of leadership which keep the organization alive and moving through consistent change and development processes. I have discovered that management is more linked to the vertical dimension of organizing and leadership is more linked to the process of organizational change and development.

In chapter three, I will show that horizontal leadership is not a person, but that it is a process of the organizational community in which we all participate. It is this process that makes things work and that enables us to understand the mechanisms. This is particularly true for the transformations of the organization and of the people in it and how we learn from them.

In chapter four, I will then move on to describe the importance and impact of the way we dialogue, being the key dimension of the leadership's ability to make the process of "creating change" work successfully. The art of creative dialoguing is outlined and how through this type of dialogue a process of organizational development and change can be initiated and can be steered in the organized community.

In chapter five, I will describe in detail the tools that can support the leadership process in practice. These tools are actually points of understanding and reference, designed as orientation in the uncharted area of leadership and organizational development in the organized community. The Sense-Making for real-life people is in this respect the most essential effect of the leadership process of creating change.

At the beginning of part two, chapter six I will describe three case stories which demonstrate how leadership in organizations has an explicit relation to the wider community. I have selected these three cases out of many more to show the connection between the organization as a living community, the leadership process that makes the organization develop, and finally the Sense-Making. This latter (Sense-Making) helps people to connect and integrate themselves in the organization, as well as the reverse, being the individual's identification with the organization and thus the alignment of one's own targets with those of the organization itself.

In chapter seven, I then move on to document the findings on the leadership process works from our institute's action research on the subject of horizontal leadership. We discovered that leadership is a very personal issue and that the people participating in the leadership process work in it with their individual insights and beliefs, which they have formed through their own personal struggle and reflective activity. There is not one single concept or model of leadership which could be generally recommended and which we can all share and apply. Each person has to make his own discovery tour in life to find the leadership as it works for him and the others he has to deal with.

In the leadership process our images of the human being are being challenged. This is what I focus on in chapter eight. What is our fundamental vision on man and his destiny? Do we only see man as an animal or do we regard him/her as a spiritual being, or how do we see man ourselves? I will be demonstrating how we can develop our own consciousness in this, how we can decide to take a personal path of development to enable ourselves to really be involved in the actual process of leadership.

In chapter nine, I will finally describe the fundamental points of view which can help us to deepen our insight and to take that personal path of researching the issues as addressed in this book. It helps us to gain a deeper understanding of the leadership processes in organized communities, of which we are a part, and hence create a sense in our life, resulting in a fulfilled and meaningful life.

In appendix two, I further detail the leadership methodology. It supports the process of our understanding on how leadership works in the organized community in practice and how it becomes effective by supporting the process of Sense-Making, required by people reflecting on their work and learning from it.

These chapters show you the main concepts on horizontal leadership and organizational development which I have published over the past years in Dutch. It gives you a good overview of my key thoughts and research findings as expressed here in the case descriptions, concepts, leadership experiences and tools.

I hope you will enjoy this book and will be able to take away the leadership inspiration to create a meaningful life in the many organized contexts in which you live and work.

PART ONE

In part one, I will explore the organization as a living community, in which leadership forms the fundamental dimensions for allowing the organization to function properly and the people, dealing with the organization, to participate in a process of Sense-Making and learning. If indeed leadership is the essential process in organizations, ensuring that all other processes work and interconnect, then we should concentrate on improving our understanding of leadership processes in organizations.

Leadership is primarily directed towards creating further development and change for the benefit of a healthy continuation of the organizational community. In order to participate in the leadership process, we should focus on how we can build our own concepts and toolbox in handling the leadership process, creating development and change.

A leadership experience:
The community banks of Germany—Sparkassen

Community banks in Germany started as local savings banks under the name of "Sparkasse". Today, the network of these individual local banks represents a complete and powerful bank organization that is strongly embedded in local communities and plays a central role in the financial market, both for private clients as well as small to medium enterprises. Each of these banks have maintained their strong link to the local community, and they act out of a community concept.

The case I am describing here is a Sparkasse with about 2,500 employees. Originally, the Sparkasse of the town was merged with the Sparkasse of the surrounding region a few years ago, leading to this impressive organizational size. Now they offer a structure with over a hundred branch offices in both city and country. Their offer covers the complete range of all financial services, which they cater to all target groups within the community. They are not only part of the regional network of Sparkassen, but of course also of the overall national Sparkassen organization. At the same time, their operations remain fully independent at their regional level.

To strengthen the common internal culture in this Sparkasse, to create a common identity in the wider community and inside the bank itself, the board of directors decided to launch a development process with the following aim:

"Strengthen the individual entrepreneurial attitude, the personal responsibility and good cooperation in the context of the whole, whilst keeping the focus on the client."

Their approach was to start this process in a systematic way, as they had discovered that the implementation of new policies was only successful when the people who have to work with them are involved in the process of creating them. The board chose two process owners as work-stream leaders, one from line in sales/marketing and one from a Central department. They had observed these two persons taking sensible initiatives in the past. It proved to be a good combination, a strong two-man team.

The process owners

"We know how difficult it is to change work patterns. Therefore, we have opted for a more practical route that was based on some key principles," said the process owners. *"In practice, our actions are limited by the existing conditions in the work space. We do not want to start to change these conditions. Instead, we look for initiatives that can be taken forward within the existing conditions. We aim to stimulate our colleagues to act in a personally responsible fashion. We help them to take small steps in a consistent way.*

To begin with, we invited seven heads from our branch offices, who were generally regarded as representing the overall average views and opinions, and we asked them whether they had examples of personal initiatives they had taken in the past year. It became clear at once that they were more used to reacting to commands from others. They wondered what it would mean to start instigating their co-workers to take personal initiatives in such a rigidly bureaucratic organization as theirs. The only real example they could come up with was that of the only female department head in the group of seven.

It had been her responsibility to speak to clients with long-term overdraft on their account. As she did not care much for this task, she delegated it to her staff in the agency. Each one of the front office reps had to monitor a short list with this type of client. She found that her co-workers performed the job much more consistently than she had done and that the clients reacted more positively to being addressed by them. By the delegation she had gained much more time to spend on other jobs, which were essential to her leadership.

She had difficulty to share her story with the others in the group, as she believed her initiative was running against the rules within the bank. However, this example triggered the group to design an initiative they could take in the next period in which they could increase the involvement of their own employees. Already in the second meeting a number of interesting feedbacks on how these small initiatives worked out in the sales offices were reported. The team leaders were in fact surprised how well co-workers reacted to the newly gained freedom that was given to them."

The young people's project

The next step in this process was that leaders of teams were asked by the process owners to select young members of their teams for a special project. These young people were asked to do a project from start to finish on their own, focusing on improvements in the relationship between the team and the client. This could be through increasing sales of a product that was not running well or improving a work process with colleagues which was over-complex and caused mistakes. They were allowed half a year to design and implement the improvement they wanted to bring about. The process was operated with groups of 14 to 20 youngsters.

It started with an opening session in which the young people and their team leaders presented their project aim to the process owners and one member of the board of directors. After some months, the young people came together to discuss their projects, the progress, the bottlenecks and the next steps. The process owners coached the young people in this meeting, and the youngsters also gave each other advice for handling and resolving difficulties. In a third and last meeting, they presented their final results. It was surprising and thrilling to see how the young people were fully engaged with this challenge and what the result was in terms of good ideas and client benefit. The cooperation between the young people and their superiors worked well because of the agreement in the project that the line manager would only coach the young colleague when asked to do so.

The final presentations were given to the regional directors, members of the board and their own immediate superiors. This was a very inspiring meeting for all participants. The general director was very curious on how the young people had progressed, what they learned from this experience and how the team of colleagues worked together in their project. The youngsters presented full of élan and self-confidence. They talked about their approach, how they had overcome difficulties and obstacles, how clients had reacted and how they had learned as they progressed. After this first round of projects the process design was implemented for the whole of the organization. Groups of young team members would enter in this half-year program. It was a simple but very effective way to develop this entrepreneurial attitude, and it gave people sufficient space for taking responsibility.

What did we learn from this way of developing?

It is commonplace experience that in organizations there is first a lot of discussion before there is action. But in this case action came first. The dialogue was based on what people had done and not on plans that should be executed.

This led to a much more positive atmosphere.

By concentrating on the actual initiatives themselves and not on changing the conditions first, it became apparent that much more is possible within the existing conditions than people think there is. All this became possible because the process owners had designed a process which was different in its nature from the normal everyday work processes. It is the daily routines and pressures that block people from taking initiatives. All it needed was some special process in which they would turn them in participative stakeholders to actually enable them to do this. It is striking how the participants in the projects did not need convincing on the advantages of dealing with the development issues in this manner. When they are invited to participate, contribute and bear responsibility for a change, most people are happy to step in. This also influences and attracts others when they see how things really start to move in the right direction. The process owners discovered that inviting to participate in the project groups and then moving forward with those having responded positively to the invitation made both process and progress flow easily. The support and commitment of top management protected them from the anxiety that would pop up once in a while when moving in uncharted territory.

Feet on the ground

After 150 youngsters had participated in one of the project groups, the process owners made a small video presentation to the members. They had filmed three of the initiatives. One of these initiatives had been taken by two youngsters in a branch office. They had started a process of finding new ways for getting clients interested in a new Sparkassen product, "saving for your pension". They had designed plastic feet that they put on the floor behind the entrance door, on which they had written "99% profit" in big lettering.

One of the two was interviewed on the video: *"One day I saw a small child in the agency jumping from one floor panel to the next one. Then I noticed that clients, too, just like the children, first looked at the floor when they came in. That immediately gave me the idea: this is a way to attract attention of clients to a new product! We ordered red feet at the PR department with the text 'savings towards your pension at 99% profit.' We did have to argue with PR at first, but in the end they came around and helped us. We put the feet forms on the floor. Clients noticed them straight away and asked us: 'What do you mean by that slogan?' It gave me and the colleagues a good opportunity to talk to them and explain the proposal in much more detail. What was the result? In two months time, sales of this product increased by 40%.*

Initially, we even had three other ideas, but they were all shot down by the experts of the central staff. However, because we were part of this process of self-responsibility, we kept on going and did not accept the resistance. And we succeeded! We persevered on this idea—and now the other branch offices are starting to order the feet."

The evaluation of the process

After some years we brought in a researcher to perform an official review and evaluation of this process. He started out with the four following questions:

- What were the actual results of these projects for the Sparkasse?
- What were the learnings, both for the young project members and their superiors?
- How did the projects affect the relationship between the bank's employees and the clients?
- Was there a continuing effect from the projects in the participating departments?

The return on the questionnaire, which had gone to all staff having participated in the projects, was impressive: 78% responded (of which 87% were working in sales/marketing and 13% working in the Central departments). Ten of the respondents were taken through in-depth interviews.

We could document the reaction of the process owners as follows:

"In day-to-day operations there is little space for personal initiatives of younger employees. One reason for this lies in line managers not allowing for sufficient space for them to develop in, another also in their hesitance or even lack of courage to step forward with their own initiative. We wanted to induce managers and young staff to actually change that practice. Initially we had to emphasize the differences between daily routines and special projects. In a project, the youngster could act fully responsible from start to finish, and the superior would only step in when asked to do so and then only in a coaching role. Line managers mostly believe that the degree of delegation to their staff is far higher than it actually is: in reality this is in fact quite limited. Some of the line managers found it not so easy to 'let go'.

The projects themselves were focused on client issues and the selling of new products. For the internal staff departments these issues were obviously linked to their support to the sales & marketing colleagues. It re-quired them to involve the colleagues and experts in the project, they had to design the appropriate steps of the process, enter into a dialogue about them, get the right decisions made and implement their idea in day-to-day business operations. That created the opportunity to learn and grow in self-esteem and self-confidence. This, in turn, could mean an important learning for life. The youngster starts to see how to deal with the complexity of the modern organization and that it is possible to take initiatives, without having to change the circumstances first."

Some bare figures
Through the research we did on the mechanisms of this process we gained some interesting insights:

92% of the young people involved and 90% of the line managers found this experiment extremely useful. The younger members of staff spent an average of five hours a week on their project and also another three hours in their private time. Managers spent roughly one hour a week on the project and half an hour in their private time. 60% of the projects actually continued after the first six months and the final presentation.

In 50% of the cases there were new projects started in this initiative taking way.

60% of the projects led to a substantial growth in client sales, and in 20% of the cases significant cost reductions were achieved. In 40% of the cases the work processes were simplified. Improvements were achieved in 60% of the cases in client relations, in 40% of the cases in cooperation between colleagues and in 30% of the cases in the cross-departmental cooperation.

60% of the cases saw a noticeable increase in identification of employees with the Sparkasse.

83% of the managers mentioned a higher level of trust and confidence to delegate much more challenging tasks to their co-workers than before, and 40% of the co-workers indeed confirmed this move.

83% of the managers expressed their intention to continue on this path, and even 97% of the youngsters were eager to continue with greater responsibility and taking personal initiatives, with the support and coaching from their line manager. 80% of the young people now actively ask for involvement and responsibility in challenging tasks.

These figures show that when we are able to connect the leadership process with the client process and involve not only a few experts but the whole community / all stakeholders to participate in this, then we can expect inspiring results. In these leadership-and-client processes lies the potential to perform creative activities in more freedom and to see a process through by taking initiative, cooperating with the others and implementing the findings in the day-to-day operational processes. To reinforce this claim, I will render some quotes from those involved in the overall process.

Some testimonials

A line manager: *"The aim of this process was that our young co-workers, who still have their future ahead of them, learn to take up and pursue issues in a mature and independent way. This strengthens their knowledge, their sense of results and how they appreciate themselves. It also leads to good results with our clients, and we see this reflected in our financial results. This also mirrors our respect in working together in a team. The youngster is not led to consider himself as the fifth wheel on the wagon but as an important member of the team, as part of the community."*

Another manager: *"It is not only about the results we achieved but also about the experience of how processes work. It is about shaping the process, taking steps, overcoming resistance and reversals, finding alternatives, that is what I find the most important result of this process."*

A young co-worker: *"I was enthusiastic about the idea to work with full responsibility and not only within a fixed frame. You choose a project that you find interesting, you work with your own ideas. You see the results and you learn from it."*

Another young employee: *"We have devised a systematic way of dealing with the market for younger clients. We have developed a rhythm, and so the work becomes more simple and enjoyable. Once we got used to the new process, we would document the most important details in the client's file after each meeting with him. Using this information in the next meeting with this client, he finds this very pleasant, as he feels respected and treated in a personal way. We do not need to each time start a discussion from the very beginning, but resume the dialogue from where it was left off at the last meeting."*

A manager commented: *"One of my young colleagues also presented her results to our own team. That improved the team spirit substantially. A good team will have an impact on the overall performance of the agency. Her other colleagues got caught up in the enthusiasm and demanded to also be assigned their own personal challenges, and the teamwork between them further improved—which again was much appreciated by our clients and resulted in an even better performance of our agency."*

A manager summarized: *"Up till now, we were a small universe of people who were led by the hand of our boss. However, our Sparkasse has grown and become more complex. Now this old model of leadership is not working anymore. Our co-workers have to work with greater responsibility. This can also be seen in individual targets set for each co-worker and how he must plan his time in advance. Our staff is also advancing in their personal development and keeps learning all the time. And I encourage them: Do not wait for the next training course! This is relevant to all of us. It is my role now to help the team to do this. I have to coach the workers much more, it used to be necessary. If I default in my new role, then the immediate reaction in my team would be one of dissatisfaction.*

The process owner: *"What I found interesting and discovered is that we had much more freedom and space to act, but also that we carried more own responsibility for our performance than before. It became clear that we depended on each other to be able to do this. The team and the leadership are essential to make this happen. It was and still is a great experience to be part of."*

CHAPTER 1 # The organization as a living community

In this first chapter I will deal with an image of organization which at first might seem unusual and can be characterized as the "organization as a living community". This image is based on our real-life experience that it is the community of people and their leadership which makes this community develop. It is their input, making the organization continue to grow and prosper. Our view is also based on the vision of some of the greatest management protagonists of our time, and I would like to start by quoting some of them:

"One and a half centuries ago, most social tasks were being handled by families," says the late economist, propagator of Business Process Reengineering and Six Sigma, *Peter Drucker, "now they are all performed by managed institutions that need autonomy to be able to perform. I dare say that the level of our civilization depends on the performance of all these institutes and their management."*

However, not only Peter Drucker calls our attention to the dominant role of organized institutions in our society, also former head-planner of Shell, *Arie de Geus*, describes the phenomenon in his book "The living company". He makes us aware of the limited perspective many managers have with regard to their organization, which can in fact create many problems or even become life-threatening. They generally see the organization as a means to an end and not as a living organism, a community of people. *"Why is it that so many companies die so quickly and vanish? There has been much speculation about the cause and a lot more research than is needed. But there is ever-growing evidence that this is due to the fact that managers' thoughts are limited to the economical facts. In other words, managers are too fixated on the financial results of the company and forget that the company is also a community of people,"* writes de Geus.

He identified four major factors as crucial for the life of organizations which he had seen at work in companies with a long history and tradition:

1. They had been sensitive to their surroundings, they learned to adapt to their surroundings.
2. They also had acted consistently and had created a strong identity, with which they had been able to build a coherent community of people and hence further foster their identity.

3. They were tolerant towards activities on the fringes of the organization; they had a conscientious and constructive relationship with other communities outside the company.
4. They were prudent in managing finances; they controlled their growth and development in an effective way.

Arie de Geus sees the consequence of all this in the following way: *"This means that managers of a living company must involve their people in the continuous development of the company... The leadership of long-established companies had a sense of community and empathy with their surroundings. This sense was not a weakness or the result of wanting to please the public by being be a socially responsible institute. It was part of the self-interest of the company."*

Not only leading management thinkers discovered the meaning of an organization being a community, also post-modern philosophers and sociologists are increasingly paying more attention to the importance of organization for society and for the individual. They see the transformation of our society from being a set of independent communities to which the individual belongs and subsequently attaches their feelings of the "self" towards a society in which the individual stands at the center and freely chooses to which community he or she wants to belong. It is the transformation of our lives from living in traditional communities such as a family, a nation, a religion, a profession towards living in organizational contexts. The organized community is seen as a social contract between free individuals. People come together when they have common interests. Nowadays, people belong to many different organized communities.

Seen from this perspective, it is good when we become aware that humanity has always been part of a development which can be characterized as falling out of the godly world, the natural circle of existence, and becoming part of a self-created organized world. Since *Aristotle* in his economic works already pointed out to us that through the exchange of goods we have actually left the natural circle of events created by the Gods, there have been substantial breakthroughs that have strengthened this process. The process of storing for later needs, the division of labor, the capacity of memory, the innovation of technology, the development of language—all have brought us into a world filled with human creations, of which the organization is the ultimate creation.

It is becoming apparent that an organization is far more than we have been prepared to accept in management and organizational theories in the past centuries.

1. The organization as an entrepreneurial being

1.1. Capital takes the helm

Today, organizations are seen as a tool for realizing specific aims. People in organizations are viewed by managers as one of their management resources, as there are categories like technology, system, process. Organizations and individuals are instruments to create an added value. They serve us as buyers, they provide us with work and a salary. The resulting financial profits are the main focus for managing organizations. The fact that nowadays we all participate in the financial interest of organizations has greatly intensified in the course of the last three decades. The guiding principle of shareholder value has becoming the foremost dominating aspect in many organizations. This has also infected a great number of organizations in the public domain. Now even non-profit entities have to be run not only effectively and efficiently but also profitably. We consider it absolutely normal that results of organizations are primarily expressed in financial terms. The investors train of thought is the predominant factor driving the actions and decisions of management. Capital ownership controls the organized world through management.

1.2. The customer and the employee

One can indeed ask the question what this means to the other two key players in the classic triangle of an organized community doing business, the customer, and the employee. In practice it means that the customer has been pushed to the end of the line. He receives the goods and services that have been produced: he has become the final stop of the entrepreneurial efforts. The employee is seen as an operator, hired to produce and/or serve. Big multinationals all over the world have been following an anorexia strategy in which they systematically cut back on the labor force to maximize the profits. The argument is that global competition is forcing them to act accordingly. However, a Dutch study on this strategy (Arjen van Witteloostuijn: The anorexia strategy) and the effect it has on these companies has shown that it is a threat to the long-term well-being of these companies, because customers and employees don't feel connected to the company anymore: there is no more identification with or loyalty towards its future left. It can ruin the outside community and lead to panic reactions from top management—sometimes even overcompensating the company's profits.

1.3. A different view on organization

People like Arie de Geus, Peter Drucker and Peter Senge offer us a different view on what an organization is. They see the organization as a learning community, in which young people can start their lifelong learning experience, in which people can set themselves to useful and meaningful tasks in life, and where older people can share their experience with the young ones. They show us the essential meaning of co-leadership.

Bernard Lievegoed presented to us in his book "The developing organization" how leadership has evolved over the last decades from an individual pioneering task to a community challenge. It started with individual entrepreneurs, setting up shop as a family business with energy and a brilliant idea that met a real need of the customer! A good and well-known example of this is Henry Ford. He had a very strict set of ideas and principles he worked towards. For him, the key to leadership was the realization of a service or product for the customer at the cheapest price possible. To realize this, he said, there should be a solid product with a healthy life-expectation as well as a constant change and improvement of the process of production and distribution. Already in his time he was aware and skeptical towards the purely capital-driven attitude of many entrepreneurs, and reading his book one can see that there has been little change in this attitude to this very day and age. According to Ford, this approach to business is the decisive life-limiting factor for organizations.

1.4. From entrepreneurs to management

After the two Great World Wars we saw leadership developing into managerial performances. The management system took over from the individual, the result being organizations only managed and driven through the interest of capital. The way many companies change hands shows us to which extremes this kind of management system can lead today's economic system.

However, this type of leadership has meanwhile attracted a lot more debate, as we start seeing the damage created to our society. Not only do we see rising unemployment and sick-leave rates, but also environmental issues, administrative criminality, governance conflicts and all-out company battles. The necessary balance between the three key factors in organizational life— capital, labor and goods/services—has been violated.

Today, the next step in leadership as an organizational category that needs to be taken is the integration of this responsibility and quality of life in the work process of many people. We can no longer leave the urgently required decisions to the "happy few" at the very pinnacle of organizations. Nowadays, every employer works independently being supported by systems. Only a few of them are fully dependant on their superiors to tell them what to do.

There has been an interesting shift in what leadership and management is about in this new phase. No longer is it leading people from the front, directing and controlling them in their activities. This task is part of the management *systems* implemented in many areas, such as production, finance, logistics and HR. Management itself is set to the task of steering through a maze of work processes, to achieve the defined targets. This means that the three key players I mentioned—the capital owner, the customer and the employee— must strive to balance their interests (see Luc Hoebeke: Making work systems better), whilst acknowledging that many other stakeholders also have their own interests and agendas which will affect these processes. An organization is *the* central point of gravitation for many processes in society and because of that, all people involved in an organization must steer their own work process in interaction with the work processes of many other stakeholders.

Let's focus here on what this development means for the leadership of a modern organization and how it relates to organizational community issues.

1.5. The process of leadership

The aim of leadership in organizations is in first instance and traditionally to create added value. By transforming natural resources into goods and services the pioneering leadership creates products. This responds to the needs of people requiring these products for their own lives and their work processes. It then becomes a key issue that in producing these goods and services the economical organization can balance the processes and link them to the market and the customer so that there is an extra added value, a profit. This profit enables to innovate and mobilize the initiative and creative powers of the people within the organization, which in turn ensures the economical long-term well-being of the company. We can characterize this as two distinct dimensions of leadership:

1. The dynamic performance of operational actions through creating a balance between the interests of the capital owner, the customer and the employees.
2. The realization of innovation and change, which are necessary to fulfill the many external and internal impulses and interests of stakeholders.

The aims of an organization

In the context of this basic view on organizational leadership and community one can identify three purposes of leadership in organizations:

1. They are to generate an added value in many different ways for capital owners, customers and employees, as well as for the many stakeholders linked to the organization.
2. They are also to create interesting and inspiring constellations of people working and learning together. Through interaction between many different people and parties with very different backgrounds in organizations, leaders are able to meet the unknown and participate in the building of society.
3. And finally they are to give everyone the opportunity to learn and develop. As individuals we meet many challenges in life, have to test and rethink our ideas and can grow by taking the next step in life.

With these three aims, which are relevant in the reality of our organized life, we create through organizational leadership a community in which human beings can carry out their tasks in life and meet fellow companions to travel for as long as they wish. Unfortunately, at the same time these aims are very often not perceived by financially-driven modern management as their principle targets in life.

2.   Seven traditional leadership principles for the process of community building

As I have already indicated several times, it makes a lot of sense to not only see an organization as a profit-generating machine, but to see organizations first of all as a living community creating an added value for all those involved in it. To get a bit more insight into the importance of an organization being a living community, we will look at "leadership principles for community building".

The human race has always strived to form communities. Communities are not only relevant for us as an individual because they give us the opportunity to mirror ourselves in the light of the community, to be observed and seen by others provoking comment or even judgment, but also to grow and develop, connect to and love others. We live in natural communities like our family, our village, region, country, our religious and professional groups. But at the same time we also live in organized communities. In these organized communities we fill in different roles, like customer or client and employee, owner and supplier. We live the organized life in these organized communities.

These organized communities have integrated a number of traditional, natural leadership principles for community building. I will try to characterize seven of them.

The *first* principle: **Inheritance**

The first leadership principle for community building is that of family ownership, based on power that is handed down along the bloodlines of a family. This leadership principle is the basis for many entrepreneurial initiatives. Even today we see that the majority of businesses in the world are family-owned companies, having originated from the initiative of a pioneer and continue to be led by a succession of family members. It is the values of the family and the family tradition that strongly influence the company culture, which is upheld and perpetuated by the leadership of the family in the company.

The *second* principle: **The idealistic ideology**

It is people with strong convictions and ideals, living in the natural community, who take the lead in a business. They are driven by a mission to share their own values with a wider community. In order to do so, they build a company that expresses these ideals through their services or goods. We can see this for instance in a lot of enterprises created by their founding fathers with a religious background, wanting to spread their ideals in the wider community.

The *third* principle: **Hierarchy**

We are used to group ourselves on levels based on the principle of hierarchy. Through the many centuries of our existence, we mortals have viewed the Godly world as hierarchically structured. In companies doing worldly business, we have taken to this principle of hierarchy. Everybody is positioned on a certain level and is given a task connected to this level. It is the power that goes with hierarchy that is working between us in organizations. It is the leadership that uses the power of hierarchy in the community to give direction to its development.

The *fourth* principle: **Group solidarity**

In our day-to-day life we tend to connect ourselves to groups to which we feel attracted, such as friends or sport clubs—we feel we belong there. Joining an organization you also meet specific interest groups with a certain style and norms you need to adopt if you are to become a part of this group. It is the leadership group that is the most dominant group to belong to and we can strive towards becoming a member of this group. You either feel at home in this group or you sense it as a strange constellation of people you do not want to be part of.

The *fifth* principle: **Role consciousness**

In the traditional community we take up certain roles. It might be that these roles could be performed for a life time without ever changing. In the organized community you can step into different roles. There is a certain authority connected with roles and they require certain attitudes. The organizational roles are very much acted out on the basis of professional standards that have to be acquired. It is the leadership role that will bring the different roles together and ensure that the incumbents of each of these roles cooperate.

The *sixth* principle: **Community rituals**

The community uses certain rituals to celebrate important moments. These rituals are enacted by the leadership with and for the community. Through these rituals we share a common experience and remember that we are part of this community. They enable us to establish our loyalty to this community and we experience an increased sense of identity with this community by sharing the ritual.

The *seventh* principle: **The personal initiation**

The individual has to internalize the discipline and the convictions that are the prerequisites to being part of this community. We need to demonstrate to the community that we have fully embraced these standards and can comply with them. In organizations we follow an individual path of personal evolution. This path is the strongest in the leadership, where we actually connect our personal biography with the biography of the company.

Studying organizations and their mechanisms, we can see these seven natural "leadership principles for community building" at work in the organization, making it a community construct. These principles give the organization a communal quality, and we become part of this community, starting to identify with it. I see these principles as vertical principles. They work between heaven and earth in the community, between top and bottom: their existence is evident, they are there and we adapt our behavior to them. Those entering in the leadership are the natural carriers of these communal principles.

3. Three developments

Today it is, however, no longer self-evident that these principles work in the same way as they did in the past. Because during the last century in particular we see three main developments that threaten these traditional community principles and open up the community to other influences of leadership. The three developments described here have substantial effects on the leadership, being carried out in organizations today.

The first development we see is that of the rise of "systems" in all spheres of life.

Our life has been "systemized". We complete all the life processes with the help and under the guidance of systems: they are the regulators for our performance in the process. We are able today to handle these systems, as they are mainly based on the technological inventions we have made ourselves. It is through this systemized world that we can individually divorce ourselves from the above community principles. We can perform our processes outside these principles. The virtual world of the Internet is an excellent example of how this works: we can live in a virtual world, not needing to interact too much with the real world we come from. We may spend more time in the Internet than playing with our children. The strongest effect of the systemized world in organizations is that the "leadership" has been transformed into "management". It is no longer the person of the leader and the leadership group that makes the decisive difference, but it is the management system that operates and guides the company. The manager's function has been reduced to controlling all the other systems which the people work with.

The second development is that of "networking".

Having generated these systems, we then can create the networking level. We all become involved in world-wide networks, since our life is connected to almost every type of existing process and organization. We participate in networks as a client, a customer, an employee, or owner. New kinds of constellations with people coming together due to their role in organizations are born. We witness people with totally different backgrounds, such as religion, color, tradition and profession networking with each other in organized communities, as they share a common fascination or interest. The natural basis for leadership has disappeared. There is no self-evident acceptance of leadership in the community based on inheritance, ownership or idealistic power. Leadership has become anonymous and it is often not clear to community members who actually is in charge of the leadership in the organization. Leadership has been reduced to a community process, in which many different persons participate and not only the traditional elite, as we were used to.

The third development is the "individualized life sphere".

On the basis of the world of systems and networking we establish our personal world of our identity. We graduate to an individual thinking. We have an intense experience and feeling with regard to our personal identity. We go our own way, which is not anymore rigidly and strictly bound to our natural roots. There is no more natural loyalty left for the leadership, we meet in organizational communities. We create our self as an independent unique composition. This, however, is often accompanied by disharmony, conflict and confrontation. We have to face our "double" and we realize what a complex being we have become. This means that the leadership connection to the organization is open to anybody who wants to make the effort to participate in it. The personal loyalty to the organization and its destiny has to be built up out of the individual resources people have and are prepared to dedicate to the organization.

Today we see the traditional "leadership principles for community building" becoming interlinked and mixed with the new world of systems and networking individuals.

4. The ascension of management

The result is a strong connection between the traditional principle of hierarchy and the industrialized principle of system building. Together they form the basis for the dominance of management in the leadership process of organizations.

4.1. The principle of hierarchy and the big stories that go with it

We are still used to align ourselves to the hierarchical structure of organizations. Up until today we have lived with this principle and each new generation follows suit. The hierarchy is connected to the power to make things happen. In order to have an understanding and an acceptance of this principle, leadership has created the big company hero stories we love to tell each other and which reflect the unique culture of which we are a part. These big company stories have an almost religious or ideological quality to them that touches the sensitive man who is trying to understand why life is like it is. The great stories are about the founding pioneer, the first steps leadership took with the community, or their victories that were experienced and the confrontations and crises that challenged the leadership in its existential responsibility for the continuation of the organization.

4.2. The principle of the division of work and the ensuing orientation towards targets

Ever since the industrial revolution we have worked with the theory of the division of labor, people specializing in small parts of the whole process. This has increased the speed in the process of production enormously and made it possible to meet the ever-growing demand levels of consumption of the world population. The array of functionalities was raised. To be sure that everything could fit the whole, management began to formulate targets for teams and individuals to concentrate on. We ended up with the management "in control" and structures of experts forcing each individual to perform their own task in a small corner of the whole, nobody fully seeing or understanding the complexity of the processes. Finally, we have arrived at a planned way of working with standardized products and processes—the community leadership has become anonymous.

These are the two dominant principles which have made us focus in organizations only on what we call "being in control" and "creating permanent
change". This is the paradox in today's management and leadership that we
are dealing with in the modern organization.

4.3. Being in control and the systems that go with it

To get our act together, the management of an organization wants to structure
and systemize the work processes being performed by people. The effect is
that each one of us is doing these work processes on our own with the help of
the systems, while communicating and interacting with many other people in
and outside of the organization on a purely functional, task-oriented basis. To
remain in control, the management and experts use an ever-growing amount
of systems. It is the technology that has helped us to create these evermore
complex systems and we have become no more than the operators of systems.
The most extreme format is the automated company, the virtual organization.
And all the while the management has become a system in itself which is expected to work as a leadership system for the community.

4.4. Changing organizations and the horizontal leadership to make
it happen

Because of the complexities we have created it is, however, almost impossible
for anyone to oversee, control and understand the whole. When we continue
to work (unidirectionally) top-down and bottom-up, when we are forced to
specialize more and more, when the processes are fully system-controlled, we
tend to loose contact with the social reality in the community. We then have
to make an effort to see through the complexities and communicate with each
other, so that we understand what is happening and why we are doing this.
This requires from us that we communicate in a more reflective way. We start
to realize that there is a permanent process of change going on. We are in fact
all part of a continuously changing organizational reality. We need a process
for handling this permanent change. The research on organizational change
has shown to us the inability of management to handle the change processes in
the context of the operational systems it is working with. We discovered that it
is what we call "horizontal leadership" that makes this change process happen
in the community. And it does not happen by itself. It is evident that there is a

growing need for new ways of leadership, of a more reflective and participative style, to be able to develop and change the organization and ourselves, to find the next step.

5. The lean, learning, and living organization

To connect with the forces perpetuating the organizational community, we have to enter in the world of change and organizational development. We need to understand that not only are the *vertical* principles and systems keeping the organization and the way it operates under control, but that there is also a great need for the principles of *horizontal* leadership, working between us in the socio-economic life. They generate both value and sense for us and guide us in the development of the organizational community and change. We see this become manifest in new, global cooperation as well as in concepts for leadership development in the field of management and organization.

Three of these new examples of the principles and concepts for applied horizontal leadership for change are the lean, learning, and living organization.

5.1. The lean organization

The "lean organization" was initially introduced by Womack and Jones and it was based on their studies of the Toyota organization. They had discovered that Toyota had introduced working in a much more horizontal way, integrating customers and suppliers along the chain of value generation, trying to "get it right first time" and in a "waste-free" way. They then published the "lean thinking book", that started many companies in the world looking at their own organization as a bundle of processes. Subsequently they had opened up a way to start to deal with these processes in a more developmental way. The people in the community were expected not only to perform their tasks but also to contribute to improvements by making their work processes more lean.

The basic idea of "lean" is:

- We create value for our client and we eliminate all that is wasted energy or repeated tasks (for instance due to errors in the process!).
- We balance capacity and process.

- We make the process into an end-to-end flow by the "pull" mechanism, that is that we respond to the client order directly rather than producing and pushing the product into the market.
- We strive for continuous perfection and "first time right" approach.

Of course, there were many organizations that used these "lean" ideas in the traditional vertical management sense by cost cutting and controlling. The real value of "lean" in the longer term, however, has to do with consciousness of the leadership process in the whole community and the dialogue on horizontal leadership that goes with it. It is the customer who needs to be at the center of all our attention and efforts.

5.2. The learning organization

The "learning organization" was first described by Peter Senge and others. They saw the need for personal professional mastership in the work process and they made us aware that this heart of being a professional was stolen by the machine image of the organization. The "learning" organization is an organization in which the community is in a permanent process of knowledge creation. For this to happen it is necessary that the company's values and principles are much more integrated into the heart and the community's awareness. That requires a different leadership compared to the one being normally performed by management in today's businesses. It is this leadership quality of creating community learning which will enable people to give personal professional meaning to their work. People who are developing themselves will develop organizations, and this happens through a learning process of self- and team development.

5.3. The living organization

We will find an example of the "living" organization described in the book "The living company" by Arie de Geus. He shows us that the continuity of an organization is mainly dependent on the continuation of the community of people. How do we integrate a new generation, how do we find the new entrepreneurs, the leading constellation of people taking the next step with the organization? To also see the organization as a community opens up the opportunity to abandon this dominant image of the organization as a successful machine only churning out profit. We can integrate the whole idea of the organization as a community in the leadership steering the organization. We are able to add more sense to what people experience in organizations, how organizations influence their life's biography and how organizations are the place in which they can change and take on the unknown.

Conclusion

I have tried to show to you that we are on the one hand confronted with the more traditional vertical organizing principles connected to management and the systems for control, and on the other hand we seek new and horizontal "leadership of community" principles, dealing with permanent, ongoing change issues and organizational development.

Over the past decades we have seen the rise of the horizontal "leadership of community" principles with the introduction of project organization, the matrix organization, and now recently the process organization. We have discovered that an organization is a grouping of communal units that follow their own processes and identity rather than a pyramid of hierarchical functions. We have become aware of the sensibility of creating self-sustaining business units, profit units, development units for which the leadership is responsible of balancing the permanent operational performance and the permanent change and development process. We have come to appreciate the advantages of front and back office processes and how they run in a circular horizontal way, connecting client questions with responding processes. We see the networking organization, the virtual organization, the value-creating chain organization. All are expressions of a development in the direction of a more horizontal way of organizing our life and our communities through horizontal leadership.

A leadership experience:
The general director

In Brazil there is this family-owned agricultural enterprise, which was started back in 1959. The founding father was a real pioneer, having built up and expanded this company with his own blood, sweat and tears. His sons joined the company some time after it was originally established. Today the family operates five companies and another five joint ventures with other companies also belonging to the family. There are 1,500 active employees and during the season another 1,500 join the ranks.

The family itself is divided into two camps: "the capitalists" and the "socialists". The capitalists see the profitability of the company as the most important goal, whilst the socialists have a greater interest in the more humanitarian issues and a socially compatible and sustainable development of the community.

The eldest son has been the general manager for the past ten years. "If we don't make a profit out of it, we stop doing it", is his motto. He focuses on investing in new land and new businesses. He has the vision that the company group will play a leading role in the market and that this will safeguard employment for future generations. Together with his brothers and other family members of the leadership group he forms the "general management circle". This circle is controlled by the so-called top circle to which also some external, non-family members belong.

Over the years we have seen a few conflicts amongst some family members concerning the overall direction of the group, but ultimately everybody stayed on, except for one of the brothers who sold his shares.

To offer the next generation of the family a perspective in the company, those interested can participate in a special trainee program. They will work as team leader in one of the companies, whilst being coached by one of the family already in the position of a director. These directors also give the new generation special challenges, which they have to see through to the end. These youngsters then act as process owners and work on special change and innovation issues together with many different employees in the company. They are encouraged to their own networks, to learn how to move horizontally through the company and test their abilities to lead and steer. This builds up the next generation of leadership.

The general manager now is surprised to see that the "capitalists" and "socialists" have left their trenches, starting to exchange their views more freely, interacting in a more constructive manner; they have begun to develop a better ability to see things from different angles and perspectives. Without paying much heed to the two polarized ideological positions—that of the general manager on profit and the other, more idealistic position—they concentrate more on the customer process and the community development process. These different dimensions of capital, work process, client and community development can come more into balance and receive more attention in the day-to-day business activities.

The general manager:

"I see this as an opportunity for myself to do my job over the next years in a slightly different way. The next generation must have the chance to perform by themselves. I need to give them operational responsibility. As a result, they gain experience business and grow confidence. In return, I have more time steering the overall group.

We are able to be more aware of who our company is working with and thus being perceived by outside stakeholders. Some examples:

Every year, for instance, we have hundreds of school students doing internships and apprenticeships in our companies.

We strengthen our links with our customers all over the world. Already now I see some good examples evolving, how in different companies they deal in their specific way with their clients. The client dynamics in the potato market, for instance, are very different than from those in the flower market.

We are starting to do more experiments in nature conservation, using different techniques in earth treatment.

At the same time the social dimension is renewed. We now have process owners proactively addressing difficult issues in the group. They have to juggle this responsibility with their daily operational business chores. I appreciate that it is not easy to do, but I see it actually work very well when the person also has a real interest in leadership and is able to involve the right people in his process. Over the next years I am convinced that I will be able to reap even more benefits from this process and then to happily hand over to the next generation."

CHAPTER 2: # Two dimensions of organizing

The transformation towards a horizontal leadership in organized communities is a very slow and time-consuming process that may encounter multiple barriers. We have become entirely embedded in our systems and practices of today's organizations and we fear that by changing to a more horizontal type of leadership we would not anymore be able to hold on to the old principles of a directive top-down leadership based on hierarchical power.

Therefore, we would here like to explore and characterize this transformation of leadership in more depth and these barriers we can run into. In order to do this, we will need to take a closer look at the leadership practice of managing and organizing in word and deed today.

1. Managers and people: The questions to deal with

Managers are dealing with people all day. They get together with colleagues, speak with their co-workers or have discussions with their superiors. Sometimes they meet clients, suppliers or experts of some kind.

But does that mean that they love people?

Managers are also very busy with systems. They know a lot about them, understand them. Managers like to stimulate the introduction of new systems with which work processes and the cooperation between people can be controlled in an effective way.

Does that mean that they love systems?

Literature on management and organizations pays a lot of attention to the expansion of management and organizational systems. This has given us an extended vocabulary of management jargon which is used daily in our companies. On the other hand there is relatively little focus in the respective literature on the development of people and communities in organizational contexts. Logically, there is also less attention on what one can call the "people's language". If there is any reflection indeed afforded to this aspect, its wording usually is again in the "system language". In the daily practice of management the usual communication follows the lines of this system language, which in

41

an actual, real life situation can prevent the immediate exchange and understanding between people just when it would be needed the most. This can be illustrated by a few management phrases that are frequently used in business discussions.

"All heads turned in the same direction."
The wish of management to have people marching in the same direction to achieve a common goal.

"We have to convince our staff that…"
The longing of management that their co-workers will follow their lead, even when it is against their own interest, principles and ideas.

"With the help of our training program we want to motivate our people to work more client-oriented."
The longing of management that people can be motivated to move towards a given goal by giving them insights through training.

"We have to solve this conflict, otherwise we have a problem."
The longing of management to have a smooth operation and that conflicts can be solved to benefit this course.

"Our results do not look good, we may have to lay off staff."
The longing of management to secure business results by tweaking workforce numbers.

This is functional management slang that is intended to ensure the efficient and effective realization of targets. Management is primarily interested in the successful and efficient existence and progression of the company. To have a deeper and more humanistic language to communicate with, the people at work would be, however, very advantageous when dealing with "people issues".

One of my manager students described it like this: *"I have discovered that dealing with human issues can be fun. Previously, I was very much focused on concentrating on the organizational and marketing issues in the work space. Being involved with people means, however, that you have to put the other person at the center of your attention. You have to be intrinsically interested in human beings to be able to be a good leader. I, for my part, find it a very attractive perspective that leadership has to do with coaching people. Unfortunately, I don't see this interest in people very much in my own superior. He sometimes asks me how I am doing, but the enquiry feels more driven by form and manners than real interest. Should I move up the ladder, I will certainly aim to act differently."*

2. The human being as production factor

In the context of organizations and management, the human being is often merely seen as a productive factor. As a consequence, the human being has been reduced to being "personnel" and respective personnel policies and systems were created. Compared to for instance financial, sales, production or information policies and systems, these policies and systems are not even placed in the center of the power scale. This is reflected in the professional status of those dealing with the human factor.

Managers tend to delegate the responsibility for the human issue to specialists. These specialists train and coach the managers in social skills, in how to lead people and how to communicate with them. They develop tool kits, instruments and systems which they try to transfer to the managers.

Still, in their own self-perception, managers seem to be more connected to the abstract business than to the people doing the business. The most extreme examples we find in top floors of large companies when putting in appearances in public. These top managers like to speak about financial data, about strategies and business results—but not about the people and the community. They are too remote from the people inside their organization, kept away from them by line managers, assistants and secretaries who settle the human issues outside their own office door.

3. The human being as a "human resource"

Managing as a profession does not appear to be seen as a profession needing deeper insight into the human being, as this might be the case with for instance doctors, taxi drivers or teachers.

Is it so that managers find the human issue difficult to deal with and try to avoid this in daily working practice?

Let us look at how in medium-sized or bigger companies human beings and the human issue are being dealt with by using human resource systems.

Human Resource Management (HRM) is primarily responsible for the selection and use of labor. It arranges and negotiates labor conditions, the rights and duties of human beings within the organizational system, and has an extensive package of rules, defining and controlling the infrastructure. Problematic and difficult individual cases are handed over to other specialists, like medical doctors or social workers. Specific cases with a psychological background, e.g. burn-out and stress, are transferred to therapeutic specialists—but we tend to handle these discretely behind closed doors outside the organization.

If in a real-life situation HRM fails, we have to take a more fundamental approach.

The psychological approach to man and organization has to start from within the organization. What is keeping the people busy, how can we influence their motivation, how do we keep them on the right track and how can we make them take responsibility for what they are doing, take ownership? While organizations have become more complex and people tend to lose their orientation inside them, we see organizations becoming increasingly accessible for this dimension of the human factor.

If this alone, however, proves not to be sufficient for dealing with arising issues, we have to even take a step further in dealing with them.

We have to start a process of organizational development. Now, there is the need for real leadership. The organization and the people have to make a move towards a change—and it is the management itself which has to take the initiative by making the first move themselves. We discover that the organization is more than just an instrument for achieving business targets. This calls for a greater consciousness and sense of responsibility for what is happening to people and the community. Organizational development seems to need a reflective process and an unusual leadership process which will take the community forward. We see the need for the emergence of a new type of leadership.

In a process of organizational development, this new model of leadership will have to explore ways to transform and move into unknown territory together with the community. The organization reinforces itself now as a strong living organism which can only survive when the most fundamental needs of people and community are met. This can happen when management is willing to review their own values and motifs and with the community searches for new responses to the challenges which need to be met in the future. The organization becomes an artificially created organism in which individuals are taking the next voluntary step. Dealing with life and the future of life in an organizational context, each individual wants to be seen and treated as an authentic person. To be able to meet this reality in organizations, managers are challenged to also become horizontal leaders. This requires a much deeper understanding of the images of the human being and of organizations in the daily practice.

4. Two dimensions of leadership and organizing

We can say that there is growing evidence that the management of an organization is not necessarily the same as the leadership of an organization. There is a growing interest of social academics, as well as with practitioners, to explore the difference between management and leadership. In our research on leadership and the organizational community, we discovered two dimensions of organizing and leadership, which we called the "vertical" and the "horizontal" dimension of organizing and leadership.

"You only see it when you discover it," the famous Dutch football coach Johan Cruijff once said.

▬ **We manage the business, work and the systems in work. This runs along the hierarchical lines, it draws on the power that belongs to the position and function which is being performed. It works vertically.**

▬ **We lead people, creating values in the process, learning together, giving sense and direction to each other. This happens in a dialogical process between people. It works horizontally.**

One can speak, I guess, of a vertical space and a horizontal space in which the organization of leadership takes place.

We now want to explore these spaces, understand how they connect to leadership, how people work in them, what is possible in them and what is not.

We first want to explore the characteristics of the vertical and horizontal dimension of leadership and organizing and how management and leadership manifest themselves in them.

4.1. The vertical space

Man, in most periods of time and culture, has primarily perceived creation as being enacted in the vertical space. There exists an "upper-world" and an "under-world". Man saw the Godly universe as one of hierarchy and functionality. Every God had its place and also a specific task in the world. This fundamental image which has been handed down for over thousands of years in the soul of the human being is not in contradiction with the more recently created scientific model which attributes everything to its fixed place in nature and believes that the whole cosmos is indeed a harmonic and hierarchically built system (Kenneth Boulding / Bernard Lievegoed). We are able to predict with great precision where the star Sirius will stand in a thousand years time (Arthur Koestler).

What we jointly create as human beings is also mainly based on the same principles of order which we showed in chapter one. The organization is erected on the principles of hierarchy and the division of labor: the consequence is that each and everybody is assigned a position and function in the organizational system. We need to do so as to be in control and to ensure that everything conceivably possible in the future will find an adequate response.

Power

This constructing principle of hierarchy that we use for all our human processes of creating and of which the organization is the ultimate result can only work when it is based on power. Man can dress himself in power like putting on a suit. Power is the force that works vertically. Power makes things happen. The force of power is connected to what we earlier called the systemized world. The system is the mechanism of power keeping the organization under control. We can see this human wonder happen every day in the many organizations we have today. Is the train running on time, is the surgery in the hospital working well, is the hotel indeed where we expect it to be, is the Internet working and is the telephone ringing? We could to continue for pages listing this human miracle. Nothing in this vertical world runs by itself. Everything is done on the basis of power and we can of course also see the many disasters which result from this, too. But that is a part of creating. Where there is activity, there are also mistakes and failures. Human creation is not perfect.

Discipline

The essential human force making the vertical power world run smoothly in the longer term is human discipline. Everybody is expected to perform their task in a disciplined way. It is people's professional discipline and attitude which make the systems work. The programmed systems help us to be in control. We can observe this in a football match as well as at the management meeting table. It only works when the people involved perform their individual task in a disciplined manner. With discipline it is possible to finetune the activities amongst each other. Technology is the ultimate expression of this human power—the *prepared* human discipline (Jacques Ellul). An apparatus works as it is supposed to work and we have to use it in the way it is prescribed. There are only two alternatives: it either works or it does not work as it should.

Management

The vertical space is very much occupied by management. Actually, it is not so long ago that we have seen the organizational tool called management emerge in the organized world (Peter Drucker). In a world of farmers and small communities it was the entrepreneur, the craftsman and the individual professionals, who—next to the clergymen—were seen as responsible and thus liberated for the spiritual and social task of creating the working community. In the ongoing process of differentiation and specialization in labor processes—which has been accelerated by the ongoing expansion of technology and the growing complexity of work processes and processes of cooperation in particular—the need for more management has drastically increased. Management is linked to running the business. It is being held responsible by the capital owners for the defining and realization of company targets. For this the management is positioned vertically in the hierarchy and as a result it tends to view and treat employees in a functional way, as the resources needed to achieve the targets. Management is continually busy with restructuring the business so that the work processes are aligned towards the achievement of the targets. This requires an ongoing tweaking of labor conditions which, in turn, also have to respond to the continuous process of changes imported from the outside world. Ultimately, these adaptations cannot completely prevent the appearance of problems; and these problems can be seen as the proof for imbalances, which require remedies. All the while, however, it is clear that prevention is better than cure.

Management loves a smoothly running organization without any problems. To get as close as possible to this ideal, management will plan activities well ahead of time, decide the right strategies for the company direction, develop scenarios for dealing with future possible events and then control ongoing operations and review past performances. Management by objectives is the most revealing system to show this. Activities of a great variety have to be coordinated, a difficult and head-cracking continuous task for management. As a consequence we will see management stuck in an endless procession of meetings and sessions.

This type of management works primarily top-down and bottom-up. Once involved in the vertical columns, you will not be eager to explore the horizontal space. The first and strongest impulse is that of focusing on the own functionality, solve the immediately pending problems, acting out the power and discipline according to the individual responsibilities and competences.

4.2. The horizontal space

The "horizontal space" is very different from the "vertical space". In the vertical space everything is predestined, so to speak, is clearly defined, almost follows natural laws with inherent limitations, which shows itself symbolically in that it is hard for us to descend through the floor or rise through the ceiling, without a specific structure or support for doing so. In comparison, the horizontal space permits us to move freely without regard to any boundaries, if we so wish. It is a space between human beings. The horizontal space is not predefined; it is not limited by definition, only by the boundaries and limits created by ourselves, the walls and doors we have built ourselves.

In the horizontal space there is the process of value creation between people, which can be generated by any type of communication or dialoguing. That is a dialogical happening. The most important process that happens in the horizontal space is the process between customer and supplier (Adriaan Bekman)—whereas the customer and the supplier are not only to be seen in the classic business context: any person offering something to another, who then will be a "taker", establishes this relationship. In this process we see the "real" value creation taking place. It is a process of reciprocity, which means that one person cannot create value in isolation without the other. Because of this, the process and its result are not fully predictable. There is an open space into which we can decide to enter and freely create a specific value together. This shows itself in the book that can be read, the train that can be caught, the dinner that can be eaten and the lesson that can be studied.

A community process

The horizontal process can take place when it is backed up by a community of people who are willing to cooperate in order to create the value in the process towards a customer. The process of interaction with the customer is a process with many interfaces in which important activities like ordering, billing, paying and delivering take place. The whole of the organization is connected to these interfaces, it is moved along by them. However, at the end of the day it is not the organization but the community of people involved who cooperate and promote the relationship. At the same time, this community process also requires a leadership process.

The continuous creating of value in this process can happen consistently when we are also prepared and open to learn together. Learning from the experiences we go through in the course of the process, reflecting on how it works and even how it could work differently and in a better way: it is in the customer and supplier interfaces where we find the best ideas for the future. Here, new impulses for change and innovation are born; I estimate that in more than 80% of the cases, new ideas actually being transformed into reality are born in the process with the customer or supplier directly involved. This learning together also happens in the horizontal space. The philosopher George Steiner describes this in a beautiful way in his book on masters and pupils. The pupils have to strive to surpass the master and the master is always being challenged by his pupils to re-create the learning process again and again in a new and different way.

Horizontal leadership

Leadership is not the same as management. Where management works vertically and is primarily orientated towards the function, we see leadership working in a horizontal way by shaping the value-creating processes. It has become self-evident that when you take up a management job, you will also have the responsibility to lead co-workers and teams. This, however, is interpreted as having the power to move people in the desired direction, having all heads turned towards the same target-oriented direction and to lay off staff who are not needed anymore or are too expensive to keep. In the practice of work life, managers do not automatically also act as leaders. Leadership I see as a process between people which is happening in the horizontal space of the community. In the process of leadership the unknown is explored; there, real learning is happening, a new idea is born, the community of people helping each other is created. Leadership is connected to community building.

As John Kotter said in an interview in 2006: *"People mix up leadership and management all the time. That has far-reaching consequences. Management means: running the business like it should be done. It is responding to expectations concerning budget and time, et cetera. That is done through well-known processes, like budgeting, planning, organizing and controlling. Management is important, especially where it concerns big companies. But it is not leadership. Leadership has to do with change. It creates a vision and gives direction and strategy. The leadership communication is trying to get all the people in a common direction and inspires and motivates people to come into a movement. In stable and perfectly controlled surroundings leadership is not that important. Management is. But the problem is that the speed of change today is so very high and therefore there is much more need for leadership. The reaction in most cases, however, is that companies respond with still more management. That is not enough. Therefore, making the difference is essential. Most companies are good in managing; few companies are good in leadership. That is why mergers and change projects fail."*

Horizontal leadership makes the organization develop, and thus the entrepreneurial quality of the organism is shaped. Every one can participate in that process of leadership, but you have to be prepared to join it. "Are you going to participate?" is the invitation that is needed for this to happen. This invitation is given by the leaders to the community.

Stephen Covey describes it like this: *"Leadership means giving direction and stimulating the emotional commitment to the company's direction and the principles. When people are committed, they do not have to be managed. New leadership has nothing to do with managing people. They do that by themselves... In most organizations there is not enough trust and the workers are powerless. We treat people as mere objects. You manage things, money, stock and systems. You do not manage people, who have the power of their own will. Without trust you do not have an open and fair communication and no emotional involvement."*

5. Four qualities of horizontal leadership

In my book "Key qualities of leadership" I once described four qualities of horizontal leadership (Bekman: Kernkwaliteiten van leidinggeven, van Gorcum, Assen). These four qualities can be characterized briefly as ways of observing, how horizontal leadership works.

First of all, it is horizontal leadership that shapes the process, in which the things can happen.

If you want something special to happen, you have to *design and create a special process* to make it happen. Where the work processes are mainly built and structured in a standardized way, to be able to produce a predictable result with the help of installed systems, it is the leadership process that deals with the unpredictable; it is directed to exploring the unknown, to research and experiment. That is why leadership is involved with processes of change and innovation, the process of organizational development. In these processes, which are specifically home-made, people are moving around in uncharted waters. They have to explore themselves how things can be done differently or can be improved, and what is working and what not.

To explore yourself requires that at times you can dialogue freely with others and reflect with them on what you have observed, what that means for the organization and the work process, and how to continue. It requires a continuous *coaching of each other.*

This investigative exploring and experimenting, however, will only work when it is linked to *a vision in development.* A vision inspires and motivates the community to continue the process and carry it further. You are curious as to how green the grass is in fact on the other side of the hill, of which you had already been dreaming. You see the point on the horizon behind which the future lies. Without a vision it is difficult to find the path.

Because the new land is without boundaries, choices need to be made all the time. The available spaces must be limited and defined by choosing the next step. There is the need for focus to be able to concentrate on the essentials. Limitations are discovered and "trespassed". It is a continuous process of *breaking boundaries and setting new boundaries.*

A leadership experience:
The department head

Till this moment in his career he had been successfully leading his department. His team leaders hold him in high regard: always accessible for them, coaching them and offering good, practical advice and solutions for their business issues. They have a relatively relaxed life.

Now the managing director of the company decides to change its structure and to transform departments and teams into a range of independent units, led by entrepreneurial unit managers. Only two hierarchical levels are sufficient in his opinion. The managing director and the former department heads form the management team during the transition period. Fifteen unit managers, reporting to this management team, are inaugurated.

The department head, three years from his pension, regards this development not as a threat but as an opportunity for himself. He coaches different unit managers and helps them to progress in customer relationship, financial and personnel management. He helps them start working with their own ideas on these subjects and together with them he reflects on the actual experiences and in turn learns from them. Step by step they jointly develop a new management repertoire. The unit managers themselves have to consider customer and other work processes, they have to lead their team and engage with their co-workers who are also required to take a next step in their responsibility by handling the projects.

The department head is pleasantly surprised, how the different unit managers take on this new role. He can now concentrate more on policy issues and design new strategies and scenarios for their business, as they are experiencing a growing competition in the market. He simplifies the flow of communication and information, chooses the parameters for performance appraisal and speeds up the decision-making process.

At regular intervals he covers for his managing director on external appointments. He is meeting new people who discuss strategic issues with him on and faces new challenges in his personal network with important customer organizations as well as research institutes.

The department head:

"It is a lot of fun in coaching younger employees as a senior manager. This gives me a good opportunity to reflect on my own experiences and make them available for others to benefit from. It is not important to tell the unit managers what they have to do. Everybody realizes that this is about customers, money and co-workers. But how to tackle a complex problem, how to handle critical situations, these are the issues we communicate about. I instruct the unit managers to first listen and observe. There is always so much more to be seen, heard and understood than one thinks possible at the beginning. I encourage them to watch how their co-workers handle their issues and how they understand the real situation they are in. You do not have to offer solutions to your co-workers all the time. You can help them by making the right choices and creating good conditions for them to produce effective solutions. What I find the most interesting aspect is seeing how a leadership team is starting to learn themselves. The operational pressure is high and encroaching on the time needed for reflection. To be able to stand still for a moment and ask yourself a question, it is most important to have some personal space for reflection. That is what I do with the unit managers. We have learning dialogues in which I challenge them to think about developments that will affect our company, how we handle them and also learn our lessons from those initiatives which had failed."

CHAPTER 3: # Managers and people:
the horizontal leadership process

Having explored the vertical and horizontal dimensions of organizing and leadership, I will in this chapter now focus on how the horizontal leadership process can come alive by the intervention of a leader. This approach will support managers and also co-workers to become leaders responsible for a good and effective horizontal leadership process.

1. The horizontal leadership process

I will give you some examples of images on leadership which managers we have worked with have and which confirm their interest in also becoming horizontal leaders.

John: *"A few weeks ago, I was speaking with an owner/director of a large technical company who had just handed over the chair of the company to his successors. He related to me how he had selected his crown princes and had groomed and prepared them for the moment of taking over the helm, and how he had communicated this internally in the company when he thought the time was ripe. He also told me how the company—after it started as a small family-owned business—had grown into a bigger company and how he believed that this development called for another type of leadership at a certain moment in the company biography. This made me think. Is there a specific date when a certain type of leadership stops being suitable for the organization? Is it up to yourself to choose the moment when your leadership is not contributing enough anymore? It could also depend on the leadership which is only needed in certain phases of the company's life. A change manager might have a shorter life span in the company then a real business man. It can be dependent on acceptance by others. They say that power can corrupt in the longer run: so, could remaining too long in the leading position be detrimental to the well-being and success of the company? But we also see examples where it is the lifetime leadership that works the best. What is it that makes someone able to keep the leadership role for so long in a beneficial way?"*

Susan: *"In the past, I have been more conscious of my role as a leader and what my influence on others might be as a result. I have noticed that my co-workers are not really eager to see a forceful leader who is always fully transparent. That is only needed when things get stuck or escalate into a critical situation. Leadership is something which works between people. Some employees might only see the facilitating role in a leader. Others might expect a leader to be confrontational and very directive. The varying expectations can make it extremely difficult for the person in the role of the leader. The leader is left alone in his process. He or she has to deal with all the emotions around leadership without real outside help. In my experience I have noticed that as a leader you have to come down to the shop floor and search for the deeper grounds of how people react to leadership. How can I deal with that?"*

Bert: *"Many men say they love football. But does football exist? They believe they can prove the existence of football because there is a scoreboard and they can talk endlessly and with plenty of emotion about the winning team—or why it did not win. And because they can pretend to be coach and drone on about the strategies needed, and the wrong calls from the referee, and all the other adversities and injustices, and why the wind was coming from the wrong direction, and players with too big an ego having failed to score at the right moment, and, and, and. Man can link a big part of their identity to the sports game. Many men harbor a second identity in this way.*

Some women love football players, too, I know. They like some players more than others. They specifically appreciate players with the smooth moves on the field. And they like players interacting together. They get their greatest thrill, though, from a team of players creating surprising patterns on the field and evidently exuding joy in the game.

So: Is the dominating leadership culture a male or female?

But it can also be done in a different way:

I am reminded of the Portuguese Maria João Pires and the beautiful documentary I saw of her: "The way to home". At some moment in her life, she longed for a place to where she could retreat, where she could be herself and did not have to respond to other people's expectations. Searching for a space that did not have anything to do with her life as a famous piano player and where the impresarios of the music business never would be allowed in. Over the years, her sceptical attitude towards the modern concept of art with its business aspects of competition, ambition and marketing promotion, which is related to show and egocentrism, was put aside and she created a refuge in which she would find space for development for her own ideas in freedom. Today, artists and students from all parts of the world come to her farm, somewhere in the wild Portuguese countryside, to take lessons from Pires and other tutors.

These are the images of how I want to see my leadership and how I want to shape it."

Dick: *"As a very busy manager, albeit with a strong sense of responsibility, it is difficult to take a step back for some rest and reflection. And even when I stop for a moment, my brain continues to work on a thousand different issues. To take a rest is something I have to learn again and give it a place in my life. Without rest, my actions start to loose sense. Rituals can help me in this. Listening, for instance, is a way to take rest. Do not only listen to the words but also look into the eyes of the other person. They mirror the soul. Of course, the best way to listen is to ask questions."*

Maria: *"I have noticed that in our organization there is less time and attention for storytelling. Being inspired by the idea that one of leadership's responsibilities also lies in "Sense-Making", I am convinced that you can only create change through inner motivation, being honest and authentic, on which a personal and credible story is based. Real leaders show themselves as authentic personalities, who have no need to disseminate quick messages and stories, but who really like to share personal experiences, inspiration and motivation."*

When managers transform themselves into horizontal leaders, they start to work with the leadership process. By creating the leadership process, the manager meets some of the fundamentals of the horizontal leadership process.

2. Fundamentals of the horizontal leadership process

I would like to list some of the fundamentals for the horizontal leadership process which I have come to regard as essential for acting out good leadership in organizations. They represent points of focus for good horizontal leadership, as they emerged in the course of the research we did, sharing with many leaders and process owners during the last years.

Fundamentals of the horizontal leadership process

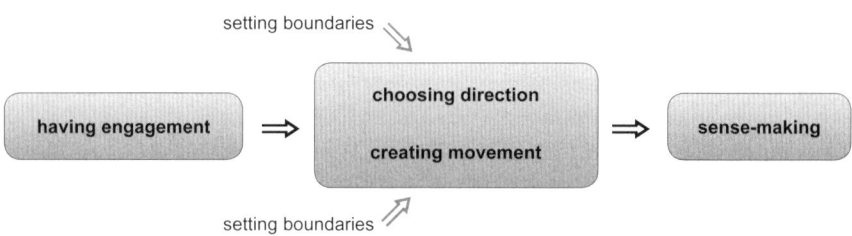

2.1. Leadership is choosing direction

▦ **"Whoever does not know the destination, cannot find the path."**

Christian Morgenstern

As already discussed earlier, we have left the natural cycle of life behind us in our organized context of life. Like Aristotle has shown us, we have entered a space without any boundaries. The goal and the direction are not self-evident. We have to choose our goals and we have to decide on the direction to take. This process of finding the goals and the direction requires a vision from leadership, a searching attitude, an intensive sensing of where things might go and should go.

The leadership can, in a process of engagement with community members, design an image of the future; it can describe possible scenarios and can make a prognosis of what might happen in the future. Real life, however, will be surprisingly different—as we know from experience.

Without concentrating on a goal and having chosen a direction, it will be difficult to actively shape the process. When people in the community do not have some kind of shared image of where to go, it will be difficult to take the same route together. These are interdependent and iterative dimensions—"the destination and the route". They surface from a constant interplay with each other. It is all about a process of searching the direction, in which we meet surprises, experience them, reflect on them and learn from them so that we can rearrange destination and route.

What helps here is to develop consciousness for the underlying values and the mission which we attempt to realize in our life. This is the moral dimension, the dimension of who and what we want to be, what we want to stand for. It helps us to make the choices about destination and route and open up to see the effects of our steps and experience the results of our own actions and performances.

2.2. Leadership is having engagement

"What is more refreshing than light? Conversation!"

Johann Wolfgang von Goethe

Leading people means being in dialogue, which means engaging and listening to them. In a hierarchical relationship it is more a unidirectional "conversation". The "senior" has the power over the "junior", because in the end it is the senior who decides. It is good for a manager to be aware that a hierarchical relationship with his co-worker automatically also leads to a vertical relationship. It is then about assigning a task to the other person, discussing work and its results, judging the performance, controlling the work process.

However, leadership can also choose to work in a non-hierarchical relationship and have a horizontal dialoguing process and relationship with the other person. The focus here then is on how to deal with customers, the professionalized work process and the quality of the work process, the cooperation with colleagues, learning together, the Sense-Making. The engagement process is a process of value generation. What one person says is nourishment for the other. Through this dialogue we create insight, we learn and make more sense, things start to get meaning for us, we meet each other, we share values, become more conscious of our own standpoint and the standpoint of the other person. We also share a vision and develop it. It is the cooperation we have with customers and suppliers and others who are involved in the organizational process which creates a positive development of the organization.

The hierarchical conversation, by comparison, is for instance an imparting of "bad news", a performance appraisal, a budget control debate, a formal decision-making conversation.

The horizontal relationship is about really meeting the customer, the collegial and reflective meeting, a meeting on vision or strategy development, the learning process.

The horizontal dialogue exercise

In a horizontal dialogue process the leader raises the right questions and gives hints for action. The co-worker might have an issue which plays a role in the work process. The leader will then prompt his co-worker by an appropriate remark or question to be able to describe and clarify the issue. The leader will ask his co-worker once in a while during the meeting to rephrase the question or issue. In the second half of the meeting they jointly explore the possible next steps. This is not about giving "ready-to-use" solutions, but helping to find a constructive way forward for the co-worker and thus facilitating the process. The co-worker will describe his/her next step, but at the same time will also retain the responsibility for the issue. The leader only will offer some hand-rails and sensible ideas for the co-worker, which might be a way forward. This is very much in contrast with the vertical way of working, where the co-worker will describe the problem and the manager will answer with the solution. In the horizontal approach there initially might be a greater sense of insecurity. However, in the end the co-worker will have gone through a process, producing not only a result which he will own as his, but also offering a learning and strengthening of the relation and co-operation in the leadership process. The leader can track the process of the co-worker and evaluate its benefit for the organizational process.

2.3. Leadership is creating movement

"Everyone is an artist."   *Joseph Beuys*

Leadership is not the same as working hard; in fact, leadership is not "hard work" at all. Leadership is more about not doing something. It is more about creating a process for others, for them to be active themselves.

Leadership is about jolting people into action and supporting the community of people to move to the next step in their personal development. This means that in the process each individual has to actually take a real step. This can be a different step for each individual. Some people get involved more than others, with a deeper and stronger contribution and trying something new. Some hit their limitations; others might step out more, having an urge to do something different. Some people make a lateral move, grasp an opportunity somewhere else and change the challenge and the human constellation of people. To propel people into motion requires inviting them to participate in the process of change and development in the organization and to start to contribute towards this. When co-workers are not offered the opportunity to participate in the process, even though they will be affected by the changes, they will not have the chance of making a personal development step themselves. Leadership means inciting people to take this step, to give them a personal and specific challenge, to bring them face-to-face with a new experience, in a new constellation of people. This helps them to develop a new field of experiences, in which they can take their own steps. By this process they can move in the changing and transforming world they are in.

The horizontal dialogue exercise

The leadership assists others in developing their own competencies and professionalism. Because people meet new challenges in their daily work, they will occasionally also experience inabilities to overcome them. What is needed then is an extension of repertoire of tools to deal with the unknown. Leadership helps the co-worker to address the issue of learning and by listening to their staff understand the issue themselves. Leadership is required to have a good command of the art of listening on the following three levels. On the first level they need to answer the

61

question: "Do I understand what the other one is saying?" On the second: "Can I emotionally comprehend the importance of the issue for my co-worker as an individual human being?" And finally on the third: "Can I sense in what direction the other person wants to move and make steps?" The leader can, together with the other person, through some reflection explore what his emotional disposition might be and how one can deal with the issue at hand. In case the matter is considered to be essential for the further development of this person in this organization, then the leader can commit to support the required process and create favorable surrounding conditions so that it might happen. This is in stark contrast with the vertical conversation, in which the manager tells the co-worker in a directive manner what he needs to learn and how he or she should accomplish this learning.

2.4. Leadership is Sense-Making

"All that we as human beings create has no sense other than the sense we add to it."

Adriaan Bekman

We are part of our natural inheritance, but we are also part of the organized world. We play different roles in this organized world. We are customer, supplier, owner, manager, consultant or any role we happen to take on in the organized process. Who ensures that all these organizational processes are aligned and come together? This is the real challenge for leadership. Not only do we manage and lead ourselves in these different processes and roles, but we can also lead others.

Participating in organizational processes costs a lot of energy. There is no natural process flow or common interaction. We have to create it all ourselves and we can get extremely involved in it. However, this does not automatically imply that it will also make sense in the end. Adding sense to what we are doing in the organized world is the final touch which is required. The car that was produced gets its sense by me driving it. The written book gets its sense by me reading it. I create sense based on the work of others.

In the individual as well as the collective world we create, there is no sense-filling experience on its own. We have to underlay our activities with sense-giving ideas and thoughts, which we can then add to what we do, observe and experience. Leadership does this in organizations by engaging on vision and mission and shaping a process of vision building. They take the initiative to involve people and create opportunities for them to reflect on what is done and how to make some sense out of it. This raises the consciousness for values and cultures; it helps to shape the moral community and gives the people the foundation for taking on responsibility.

The horizontal dialogue exercise

In the engagement the leadership tries to project the vision, which can inspire and lead community members to think about their own work in process terms, their role in these processes and how the style of working is attuned. The vision includes aspects of the goals, the common tasks and the role of the individual in the whole. It is important that the vision is clear, concrete and specifically focused. What is appealing and what is not? To describe the vision every time in a slightly different way or adding further details will keep the vision development process going. The community members can co-create in this.

2.5. Leadership is setting boundaries

"The master asserts himself by the appreciation of his limits."

Friedrich Schiller

Leadership shapes conditions and defines boundaries. Leadership can create boundaries of different kinds and in doing so will mould the infrastructure. An important aspect is the mind-set of the community's members. Goals and targets, policies, strategies, vision and mission form such a mind-set. They constitute an orientation point, a spot on the horizon, a path we can follow, a beacon on our journey, a land map.

Another aspect of the infrastructure is the physical, material infrastructure: the work areas, the technologies and instruments that are available, the systems we work with, etc.

The most forceful infrastructure is determined by the roles we take. Who is the project leader, the expert, the target group, the decision maker and the formally responsible person?

Work processes also form an important infrastructure for the co-workers, as they move and act according to them. The cycle of events in time, the flow and the customer focus give the work process its sense and direction.

By creating such infrastructures, the leadership gives the community a horizon to head for and supports the people in taking the steps so that they can be part of the whole.

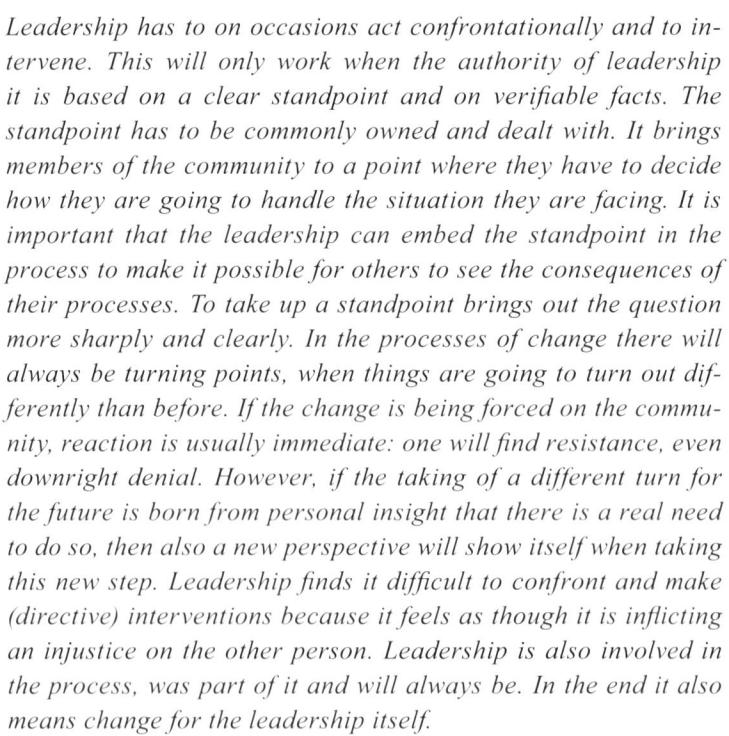

The horizontal dialogue exercise

Leadership has to on occasions act confrontationally and to intervene. This will only work when the authority of leadership it is based on a clear standpoint and on verifiable facts. The standpoint has to be commonly owned and dealt with. It brings members of the community to a point where they have to decide how they are going to handle the situation they are facing. It is important that the leadership can embed the standpoint in the process to make it possible for others to see the consequences of their processes. To take up a standpoint brings out the question more sharply and clearly. In the processes of change there will always be turning points, when things are going to turn out differently than before. If the change is being forced on the community, reaction is usually immediate: one will find resistance, even downright denial. However, if the taking of a different turn for the future is born from personal insight that there is a real need to do so, then also a new perspective will show itself when taking this new step. Leadership finds it difficult to confront and make (directive) interventions because it feels as though it is inflicting an injustice on the other person. Leadership is also involved in the process, was part of it and will always be. In the end it also means change for the leadership itself.

3. The horizontal leadership process at work

I have asked myself the question: What is the specific leadership gesture which makes the horizontal leadership process work and that can be observed in the leadership process within the community? Can we find the archetypal leadership gesture in the horizontal leadership process in an organized community?

3.1. One can discover two archetypal gestures ...

... from observation which the horizontal leadership makes all the time when it is interacting with community members. The first gesture one can characterize in three steps:

connect to what is specifically observable in the here and now

start engaging the people involved

mobilize the will and take the next step

Connect to what is specifically observable in the here and now
The leadership process will always start from what can be seen and felt in the here and now as observable and experience. Leaders will rather tend to react to actual reality than to the abstract, non-factual sentiment of what an issue might be. The concrete happenings, the actual situations one faces are being transformed by the leadership in the engagement of community members in the process. By this process the matter becomes visible as an issue and experience in the community. All involved in the meeting are helping to make the matter become visible as an issue, which we can call *"imagining the question"*. A leadership technique that one can see at work in reality can be described like this:

Leadership will concentrate on the real-life examples which clarify the issue in practice, and analyze them with the help of questions such as: What did the place look like, what was happening, who was there, what was said, what was moving the people emotionally who were part of the situation? By working through these questions and documenting the results, the issue/question starts to emerge properly for us to get a better understanding of it. We can connect to it and start to grasp what it is actually all about.

Come into dialogue with the people involved

We communicate with each other and thus give the issue an existence. This is a process of judgment building between people. Everything that is being described as a part of the appearance of the issue will start to come alive in the broader picture. Everyone participating in the process *will be inspired* to take the issue forward.

A common leadership technique one can witness in practice can be described as follows: the leadership analyzes the observations and characterizes them by a picture, and on the basis of this picture tries to understand the driving forces, the steering convictions of the people who do it in this way and not in another way. The drivers and motives of the people involved, who want to act differently, need to be mobilized in the process of handling the issue. The issue lives in the soul of the people as something they want to change and develop further.

Mobilize the will and take the next step

Leadership will appeal to the responsibility of the individual to continue the process and make next steps impacting on the issue. The issue can then develop and transform itself. It transcends to a different level of consciousness and action in and between the persons involved. Real people connect existentially to the issue and by this they also progress with their own development as an individual. Everyone becomes active in the process and will be driven by intuitive actions.

The leadership technique, which can be seen applied in challenging people all the time, is the key question: What is *your* next step?

The issue will not disappear in the abstract realities of people's mind, but will be alive in the reality of the organization.

3.2. The second leadership gesture...

... I will characterize as a process of research in which the leadership, based on results of the taken steps so far, tries to improve our understanding of the issue and the process so we can learn from it. In this instance, we can also describe three process steps:

observing the effects of our actions

sharing and balancing the different experiences;

getting common insights.

Observing the effects of our actions

If a step has already been taken and good intentions have been transformed through action into real effects, we start as leadership to see the results in practice. What were the key factors that created this effect and how can we embed these effects sustainably in the process? The mechanisms actually used can be different from the intentions we had initially. Hence, it is valuable to examine this question and try to understand the reason behind any deviation from the original plan.

A well-tested leadership technique is to focus on the actual effects in the process as well as on how the people involved in the activity were personally affected. All individuals who were part of the process will always have different observations and reflective interpretations. It is important to deal with these differences and use them for the learning process.

Sharing and balancing the different experiences

The different individuals will judge and interpret the effects in various ways and it is good to discuss these deviating viewpoints with each other. We all have formed our opinions and should share them. The process of debating what actually happened and how it turned out makes a balanced judgment in the community possible.

A technique that can be used by the leadership is to ask the participants to interview each other and try to understand how a person came to a specific conclusion. There is always a connection between what a person's present view is and what his starting point might have been in the past. But there also is the connection between what people say and were they want to go. In the balancing it is to find the common denominator of what we can learn together, without having to concede an important personal view and standpoint.

Getting common insights

By seeing the effects and spreading the conclusions in the community, we can start to learn and develop our own insights further. What is the sense of what we are trying to do? We have the opportunity to create sense out of it, to give it a certain direction. This learning process increases our knowledge.

Another effective leadership technique is to look for the images and concepts which are linked to the issue and have an inherent, simple wisdom. With these images one will assess the process from a certain perspective. It then not only becomes an individual issue but rather part of a more general insight, which unites the people dealing with the issue.

A leadership experience:
The factory

In 2001, I was invited to present our methodology to a group of social scientists and entrepreneurs in Italy. This group had been working with the question of how an enterprise, as an organized community, can be further developed in a responsible and sustainable way. The methodology seems to have a lot in common with how in the past Signore Olivetti had transformed his company into a living community, focused on development and innovation in all possible areas. Out of this first encounter a process was initiated and a number of different workshops for entrepreneurs, managers and professionals were organized. A young entrepreneur participated in one of these workshops. He was the vice-president of an industrial company and managed its parent company. He had been trying to change his company, but in his opinion, he was failing. He believed the presented methodology in the workshop could be a last chance for him to succeed.

The vice-president

The vice-president is in fact the son-in-law to the influential and powerful owner of this enterprise, consisting of four companies, two of which had been taken over in the previous years. Some of the family members, occupying influential positions like sales, finances and production management, dominated the company scene.

The father-in-law is looking after sales and marketing, seeking for business opportunities in the market, whilst he is also the patriarch of the company and his will is law.

The vice-president feels both impotent and that for the past three years he has not been able to make any substantial contribution to the enterprise. "I have been sleeping for three years," he says."I have lost my drive and inspiration."

The situation

The vice-president joined the enterprise after having worked for a multinational company out of its UK head office. His father-in-law appealed to him to join the family enterprise. He was needed, he said.

Three years had passed and what had he been allowed to contribute? All power lay in the hands of his father-in-law. The four companies produce parts for electrical motors and all four companies are in serious difficulties. Although new customers are still being attracted and new orders are coming in, there is also a growing number of dissatisfied customers. Work processes stagnate and there are frustrated managers with a malcontent workforce, unstable profits and a drastic rise in costs.

It is now that the vice-president decides to make a move.

First he formulates three key questions:

- How to reposition family members and directors in the four companies, based on their skills and competences? How to create a clear difference between ownership and leadership?
- How to force management to cooperate with each other and jointly address the urgently pending problems?
- How to improve and stabilize the profit situation and safeguard a long-term investment policy?

In many discussions with owners / family members, directors and managers he explores these questions and decides to create a systematic process of organizational development, supported by a consultant working out of the horizontal leadership methodology.

The greatest threshold for the vice-president is his own anxiety about taking the helm and confronting his father-in-law with this new and different approach.

Two images

After having taken the personal decision to move forward with his plan, he creates two images:

1. The first image is structural: four senior and four younger family members form the newly founded ownership board. At this board the targets, policies and investment decisions are being taken. The four older family members each preside over one of the companies with an advisory role. The operational leadership, however, is given to one of the younger members who act as directors together with some other non-family directors. These directors develop the strategies, run the day-to-day operations and lead the change and innovation process. Each director works with a management team in which unit managers participate. They lead the company and work together as a team.
2. The second image concerns the steering of the change processes in the parent company by decision makers and process owners. The vice-president takes on the role of general director of the parent company. This is the oldest company existing in the group with some 450

employees. Together with his unit managers he launches a change and innovation process. Operational issues are tackled systematically and—in parallel—the necessary changes are implemented by the management itself within the context of especially designed processes, led by selected process owners. These process owners are assigned to issues such as cost saving, budgeting and work process improvement.

After a three-month struggle in promoting this new structure and way of working the key players agree to give it a try.

The vice-president now finds himself in a radically changed situation.

"My father-in-law is the president and he has decided everything up till now. He sees me as his personal assistant. Now I have decided to act out of my own responsibility in a systematic way. Each week I meet my management team and we discuss issues like customer service, cost saving, work process improvement, changing the constellations and the teams.
I have now put several teams to work on the changes needed. I fundamentally restructured the company. We now have clear-cut units, each with their own leaders. We redesigned the whole process from selling—ordering—planning—producing—to delivering. We addressed and resolved the bottlenecks in the flow. I now hope that by implementing these changes we will be introducing a better rhythm into the company. So far, permanent pressure and hectic stress situations were the daily order. This would have led to disaster in the end, had we not succeeded in our changes. My father-in-law is trying to understand my different way of working, but it is hard for him. However, now we can handle his erratic and emotional eruptions in a better way. When all our managers start to work in a systematic way, we will have a better work flow, a different consciousness and a higher internal security."

The next steps
In the organizational development process many interventions at the level of the work processes are made step by step. These interventions are done in a reiterative fashion, involving all relevant people in the process of change, giving them individual challenges and inviting them to contribute.

Situation 1

The initial situation: The parent company services hundreds of customers in many countries in and outside of Europe. Each customer is treated in a similar way. There is no difference between bigger and smaller customers and there is no insight into the individual customers' unique values. Ten percent of the produced goods have to be reproduced due to faultiness. Twenty percent of the deliveries are not on time or do not meet the correct specifications. Customer complaints are handled at random and arbitrarily.

The action: Customers are segmented into a "boutique" and "supermarket" category. Boutique customers place smaller orders, however, with special unique specifications. Supermarket customers buy large volume products to standard specifications from stock. For both categories of customers a separate process is designed, starting from sales through planning and programming, production and construction towards delivering and transport. For each client there is a three-month forecast as well as a one month planning program, in which customer orders and machine specifications are linked together.

Situation 2

The planning and programming department is in a very bad shape: planning is incorrect and/or off target, there are tensions with all other departments and there is a continuous change in customer priorities.

The action: The department head is forced to leave because he is not willing to tackle the problem himself. The director's assistant takes over responsibility. He designs a new planning and programming process. He links customers' demands to machine capacities, improves the cooperation between colleagues of production and tool shop and starts an intense cross-functional collaboration with the sales force. IT specialists develop a monitoring program that helps to see where the customer orders are in the sales cycle.

Situation 3

Two young employees develop a customer / product / cost calculation program. For each customer they can now produce an added value calculation. This supports sales in negotiations with the customer.

The action: In each customer negotiations the program is used by the sales staff.

Situation 4

The initial situation: A reorganization for transport and warehouses of incoming and outgoing goods is urgently needed. All sorts of material is placed at random in different warehouses, without appropriate records to document their location. Products, having been completed years ago, are still on stock. Raw materials are chaotically ordered and delivered, without any apparent system to control the movements. Necessary internal relocation of goods is overwhelming and stifling. Transportation of final products meets changing priorities all the time.

The action: Warehouses are completely cleared of non-usable stock. Transport is brought into a systematic scheme that coordinates delivering in and outside of Europe. Standard products get a standard packaging. Contracts with hauliers are renegotiated. On-time delivery is up to 100% for boutique customers who confirm the service level agreement. Standard products meet agreed standard delivery targets.

Situation 5

The production requires a complete reorganization. It is running on a three-shift scheme. Production staff is loosely linked ad hoc to machines. There are four hierarchical levels working in the production organization.

The action: Machines are grouped according to production lines and for each group there is a team of operators assigned. Each team has a supervisor/ foreman. Each shift has a shift supervisor. Teams are informed about upcoming production targets. Tool shop workers deliver the tools in time for the production. Operators are being permanently trained to avoid machine breakdowns. The results of all teams are documented on a special wall. Foreman get specific leadership training after being selected based on their personality and craftsmanship.

Situation 6

A shake-up plan is introduced to reduce personnel numbers. The number of workers had been increased, but production levels had been lower. Now the market has become tight and material costs are up. Costs for personnel have to be reduced. The proposed reduction will affect 50 employees out of a total of 450. Various ways of handling the matter are discussed with the managers: early pension, non-performing personnel moved out, outsourcing, less hierarchical levels, reorganization and work process simplification. Existing, realistic opportunities are analyzed. After one year, 50 jobs were in fact eliminated through a combination of different methods. At the same time, production performance was improved. Individual employees are supported in the research for their next job and they do actually succeed. The initially skeptical labor union representatives are surprised how well it worked out in the end.

The action: For each of the 50 employees there was an individual solution found.

Situation 7

A budgeting and cost saving system is designed and implemented in only one month's time. Each manager receives a budget in which all financial data he is allowed to influence are placed. Each manager is asked to look for cost saving opportunities and implement them with their team. The budget system monitors the money streams on a monthly basis. Decisions to influence are made within one year and implemented.

The action: On the basis of concrete budgets, managers started to follow the financial data and made interventions to control the situation.

Situation 8

No leadership training and coaching has ever been done before. Key qualities of horizontal leadership were introduced to the managers and experimented with. These qualities were:
- steering the process,
- coaching the people,
- inspiring through a vision and
- making interventions and setting boundaries.

The question was raised: What makes a good team? And how do we become a good team? Work process improvement techniques were introduced. The biographical connection between person and organization, the connection between the personal life impulse and the company impulse was explored. This all intensified the process of knowledge creation and leadership.

The processes as described here were monitored each month in the two-day development process meetings together with process owners and unit managers. The next steps were prepared, results were monitored. There was a continuous process of steering and guidance needed from the general director.

The cultural bottleneck became very apparent in the way they each dealt with the changes. Managers and employees struggled with the given responsibility. Their mental space was not at all prepared and laid out for the changes. Through a systematic rhythmic process of repetitious exercizing in the first year, slowly the consciousness arose that this new way of working is based on different steering principles than previously, as before these had been initiated by the old pioneering generation. Over a longer period, these two sets of steering principles clashed and generated a high tension in the company.

In the course of this process, the vice-president developed a more personal strength to take on responsibility for family issues, ownership issues and management issues. He became more visible in the company, tackling the real issues in the company right down to the work floor and developing the skill to introduce a systematic way of managing change and development, all the while creating next process steps.

CHAPTER 4: Leadership and changing organizations

We have explored the organization as a process and a community and then introduced the process of horizontal leadership. In this chapter I would like to show you how the horizontal leadership is connected to changing and developing organizations.

We will first look at the leadership creating change and what makes change really stick. We found out that when management deals with change in the same way they deal with the operational issues, then the change process is not going to work. It needs a horizontal leadership approach to implement change in the organization. To conclude this chapter, I will summarize the key findings we discovered in researching this issue of leadership and creating change in the organization.

1. What is change?

Changing is more than simply improving something. It means creating different patterns, visions and another way of working. We all know how difficult it is to change an old routine. It takes real will power and discipline to do something in a new and different way and also being prepared to reflect on it permanently. One could say that change issues are only attached to the organization. On the one hand, change means integrating new elements—in the way an organization operates, as well as in the structure of its institutions. On the other hand it also involves the taking of initiatives by those who feel responsible for bringing the change about.

For now let it be enough to say that leading a change (initiative) means in my view creating new patterns, new ways of working and a renewed vision on the future path of the organization. It is a search and initiative-taking process. In this part I will now try to characterize the key leadership aspects of creating change in more depth and detail. First I will describe some processes one might find in the mainstream organizational day-to-day operations, which are designed to be change processes, but in fact very often turn out to only be an extensive "run & maintain" process. I will then move on to discuss an alternative way of leadership and changing organizations.

1.1. The need for changing the process of change

The commonly applied organizational practice can be characterized. The following example might give you a flavor of a typical course of events of a completely usual organizational business outfit:

"A problem arises in a company—for instance, some key customers are dissatisfied with the company's service provided to them. They start complaining, catching top management by surprise as they believe to have solved these kinds of problems by the internal memo they had sent to the managers in charge of 'customer quality service'. Top management now decides to take the issue more seriously this time. They call for a steering committee and one or more project teams to tackle the problem. The steering committee is chaired by a senior manager and involves some responsible top managers and a few specialists. The project team is lead by the marketing manager and functional department heads and some more specialists are nominated by the board to the project team.

The project team starts its work. First it performs an in-depth survey of customer complaints. They interview all sorts of people who might be involved. After many discussions and meetings—also in the steering committee—the project team writes and submits a report. This report is first discussed in the steering committee and then in the management team. The report lists many recommendations made by the project teams. Management decides to pursue eight of the ten recommendations. These recommendations are handed to the department heads and they are now asked to implement them. Whilst some department heads have been expecting the results and start to act immediately, others don't regard the implementation as their first priority and hence add the report somewhere to the agenda of a departmental meeting at a later date—or even let it 'slip' into the drawer.

After a while, the steering committee notices that some have taken actions, but that others are not doing anything about the report and the subsequent action points. The steering committee recommends a more directive approach from the top. Interestingly, at the same time the management team just decided to launch a general program to reduce costs. New teams are being installed to analyze activities of departments and they are asked to come up with recommendations for saving costs. Department heads, previously involved in 'improving customer service' and engaged in a 'total quality improvement project' for their own department, decide to stop this activity temporarily and now concentrate on the program for cost reduction.

Unfortunately, the management development program which the management team had agreed on—furnished with recommendations from the

78

personnel manager—has absorbed some of the promising junior managers, who consequently have little time to contribute to the cost reduction program.

As you can understand, the customers—who, initially, were unhappy with the company's service and were expecting some improvement—are now becoming restive!!"

I have seen this little story evolve in many variations over and over again in organizations and it does show that bringing about change requires more than top-down performing steering groups and project teams at work, trying to use business channels to bring about change.

1.2. Three key factors for the change process

In the practical environment there are three key factors which need to be addressed properly for a change process to successfully bring about the desired result in the end:

First of all the change process needs to actually respond to the customer's needs and not remain within the organizational framework. One of my clients pointed out to me: "All we have realized up till now is that we have shifted basic problems to other places in the organization."

The second factor is to involve all employees, who have to bear the consequences of the change in their work process, in the change process itself. What only a few might have designed and tested from their own perspective is not necessarily transferable to all others. Change has to be taken up individual by individual.

The third factor is to ensure that systems meet the requirements of the change process and the new performance targets of the organization. You can often see that this is not the case, even for some of the most modern information systems. The development of systems increasingly dictates the speed of change.

How can we take care of these key factors in managing the organizational change processes?

2. Leadership process dialogue to make the change happen

To implement change, there is a need for horizontal leadership, which pays special attention to the cooperation in the process of the community in which the change is to be brought about.

The key word for characterizing the way of creating the change is "process dialogue".

A process dialogue can be described as a way for leadership to realize change and innovation in order to get to a new performance.

What then are the key qualities of this way of horizontal leadership creating change?

We see six different qualities in horizontal leadership creating the change process.

The *first* is **creating the architecture** in which the change is realized.

The *second* is **analyzing the change** issue through the involvement of all key players and making it a business issue.

The *third* is **experimenting with new insights and ideas** to create a new practice.

The *fourth* is to **create an engagement process** concerning decisions and involving all stakeholders.

The *fifth* is to **create lean work processes, a learning community** and an inspired leadership vision.

The *sixth* is to **install a permanent tracking process** by observing results and taking corrective actions.

2.1. Creating the architecture

To realize a change that will take an organization to the next level of performance, we have to create a special architecture in which this change can evolve. The architecture is the common language we develop, use and explore to bring us together in understanding the change issue and help us to interpret the phenomena. However, not only must we try to share a common language. We also have to be more explicit concerning our internal thoughts, feelings and intentions by expressing them in images, stories, concepts and models, clarifying what we mean and see and want. To be open about these aspects shows us the differences the people involved have in their interpretations and also their motifs—in the end it will help us to find a common ground, which supports the change to come true. To take responsibility for making it happen, there is the need to clarify the roles people fulfill in the change process and in which way they have to cooperate in their roles. The roles of the participants in the change process should or even must be a different constellation than the functional constellation on which the normal operation in the organization depends.

2.2. Analyzing through communicating

Getting the key people in the process to interact openly, so that they can begin to see and understand the change issue, is the art of horizontal leadership. We have gotten used to a management expression in which management, with the help of specialists, first makes a rational analysis of the facts they see in front of them. Then they will plan for action through the existing functional structure and communicate with the people in the traditional company language. However, in change processes this leads to a high rate of failure. Resistance in the organization and structural barriers will obstruct the change process. It is necessary for the leadership to engage in a process of creative dialogue with the most important people involved in the change process, to jointly understand and be able to promote it: What are the key factors in the change question, what are the observables and what are the desired results in terms of change? Through this dialogue we start to improve our grasp on the real issues and will identify the people who have the courage and the competencies to start to advance in the change issue.

2.3. Experimenting with new ideas

In the process of analysis just described we will uncover good and creative ideas. However, simply turning over these ideas intellectually is not enough, we have to also put them to work! We can do this by testing them and measuring the results, first by experimenting with new stories, images and models and then by creating new situations to explore and practice them. In this process of experimenting we will bump into the obstacles and thresholds which then will obstruct our performance. By trying out different ways of dealing with the change issue, we open up new opportunities for realizing the change that will lead to a better performance of the organization and the people in it. We start to see how we could change the processes, how we could change behavior and how we could change our cooperation in order to fulfill the future needs of our customers and other stakeholders.

2.4. Decision making involving all stakeholders

As there are many people involved in the change who all have an influence on how things turn out, it is fundamental to get them involved in the decision-making process. When people are not involved in the decision-making process they will not involve themselves in implementing the change or will not perform in a different way. The process of decision making requires a creative process of judgment building in which the new stories and images that were created and practiced enter, thus discovering the pros and cons of the proposed changes. This process of decision making is a continuous process in which the key people communicate together. It is the leadership that takes the lead in this process and makes sure that there is a permanent invitation to participate and contribute. This helps us to make the inner shift and to accept the change.

2.5. Creating lean and learning processes

In order to enter into new performances, we have, in the end, to alter some of the existing work processes. In the change process we will have identified the critical elements, which should be placed at the center of the work process, whilst we got rid of process activities we do not need anymore. We have found new standards and criteria to help us perform in a more effective and efficient way. If there is no proper and smooth flow in a work process, we tend to get frustrated and will not wish to commit ourselves. A good end-to-end work process which responds to the customer's needs gives us the opportunity to demonstrate our abilities and our competency. A learning community can help us to challenge ourselves with a new situation and start a learning experience directed towards the development and application of new standards. The leadership can inspire us by exploring with us the decisive values and by linking the change issue to the key strategic issues, which will enable the community to achieve the agreed targets.

2.6. Observing results

To master the complexity you meet in the process of change and to get to new performance levels, it is necessary to monitor what is happening and to review the results achieved. One can very easily be mislead by biased observations.

The observations can be related to discovered numbers or figures, detailed information, statistics, pictured situations and documented events. Looking in the mirror helps us to wake up and take the right actions in order to make progress and reach the desired outcome.

By creating change processes in organizations, leaders will strengthen their link to the organized community. This ultimately enables them to make a more existential commitment and significant contribution to the organization. Leaders can learn and develop themselves in a way which would not be possible in the traditional community. The organization becomes a playground for modern learning and personal development for all. It is important for the development of individuals and the whole of society that we have the courage to continue on this road and make organizations into living developing communities.

3. A summary of the findings of our research on creating change

In the many cases I participated in, I clearly experienced that there is a direct relationship between the change issue which was raised and has come alive in the organization and the specific people within the organization who can pursue this issue. I call this "destiny leadership".

In my projects I often run into the question: "Who will be carrying this change process?" Very often the top leaders believe that the departmental head, who is responsible for matters closely linked to the change issue in question, should be charged with the task. Subsequently, experts from other departments are nominated to the project group. Already this procedure in itself makes change difficult, because the existing hierarchical and functional network is asked to carry the process, although it will almost certainly be affected by the necessary change process.

To find the right participants as contributors to the project, I often use the tool of asking the top leaders, who they see as process owners who personally qualify for taking up the responsibility in the change process. I ask them to write down one or two names on paper. In most cases, they immediately note the name of the same one or two persons, in whom all or most of the top management have confidence. It is quite obvious to me that a person and a change process belong to each other.

In the many years we participated in change processes in organizations as being part of the horizontal leadership, we have discovered a few more critical and essential points for making the change happen in reality. I will briefly summarize these points here:

Change processes stemming from the process with the customer and which are under pressure from external developments will be those with the greatest effect on the organization and the way it operates.

Change processes resulting from the organization's internal problems and/or conflicts, however, will often render management insensitive to the real changes required.

When developing organizations it is better to take little steps and actions which are directly related to those issues the client experiences in his own process.

Change processes require change process owners who lead in the change process from start to finish, from idea to reality (based on their personal abilities to do so). They are supported by experts who understand the content of the matter and are able to transfer this knowledge into practical advice and workable systems.

The clear definition of roles, transparent competencies, responsibilities and intensive cooperation between participants accelerate the change process.

The normal ways of steering change by steering committees, project groups, work groups afford little space to allow the changes to happen. Change processes require a different way of cooperating with a different set of rules.

Having a clear, shared goal, having cooperative networks of people, creating transparent time limits and mobilizing tools and money are—next to the complete commitment—essential tasks for change leadership.

Changing not only means changing organizational conditions, but also changing the ways in which the people involved work, as well as changing and redesigning the work processes themselves.

A leadership experience:
"A new director takes the lead of the institute"

After the former director of an institute was made to leave following a series of differences with a colleague, the institute was left without its leadership and a power vacuum ensued. The supervisory board asked a former member to fill in this space. This suited him well, as he was finding that his job as a banker was more and more leaving him dissatisfied. After some weeks of orientation and getting the feel, he becomes aware of the fact that the general situation at the institute was a good sight more desperate than he had initially believed: staff fluctuation was higher than 25% per year, the sick-leave rate was higher than 20%, the internal structure was unclear and everybody was only following their own whim. External partners were also not happy about the cooperation. The institute's reputation is at stake. There are only a few individuals keeping the institute going by their reputation in the outside world. The new director decides to start a process of "back to the roots" by reconnecting the institute to its original ideals and motifs.

He devised some key questions:

- "How can we renew our positive links with our financers?"
- "How can we create a lively community of committed employees?"
- "How can we re-launch the constructive cooperation between departments?"
- "How do we restructure the organization?"

For each of these questions, he selected and nominated a process owner. These process owners were assigned the task to engage their colleagues and organize them into teams to come up with answers to these questions. All their co-workers were invited to make personal contributions.

At first, the members of the supervisory board were skeptical. Each had their own personal links to the institute's staff, and they tried to influence their contacts to focus on what they thought was important. This obviously created some loyalty issues. However, the new director broke through this pattern and managed to keep the supervisory board at bay.

Once the process owners had started moving and returned some surprising and encouraging initial results, the director decided to approach the restructuring of the institute. He formed new teams, which would be asked to work on specific processes. Each team had a team leader. He meanwhile had created a management team, and the members of this team coached the process team leaders on how to make the work processes flow smoothly, how to cooperate effectively with each other, and how to achieve results. This process improved the clarity on everyone's role and position: you belonged to a team and had a clear work process to perform. The teams mostly worked in project mode, whilst a project steering committee monitored their progress and facilitated their cooperation.

After one and a half years, the sick-leave rate drops below 5%. Both the general atmosphere and the team spirit have improved to such a degree that staff retention in the institute has reached completely satisfactory levels again. The management team now steers the institute towards new challenging goals.

The director:

"I have been on the supervisory boards of various institutes like this and have witnessed how they can get themselves into trouble after a few years. It is obvious that it isn't easy to keep the impetus and stamina of such institutes alive forever. At the beginning, you might attract some very enthusiastic and idealistic employees, but after some time they risk to get frustrated by the complexities, and they can actually burn out. It is not enough to only rely on the people's inner drive; you also have to create an intelligent organization surrounding and supporting them. For me it is most important to stay connected with our external stakeholders, who have a great interest in the well-being of this institute and its work. We have a great goal to achieve that is inspiring for the wider community. We are part of a world-wide network. But it does not happen all by itself that the energy levels remain high and the roots remain intact. You have to nourish the roots, care for the relations, and connect to the others, show your interest.

We almost got wiped out by our own arrogance and over-confidence. It is not enough to have good intentions; we have to look at the internal processes to see who we are. We need to be critical about our projects' results. Is the world going to be a better place because of our work? We have to cooperate with many others to ensure that this actually becomes true."

CHAPTER 5: Tools for leadership to create organization development and change

Process owners as leaders for change can use key tools in the organizational development process of the organization. In the following, I will discuss a number of tools, each for a specific way of working by the change process leader in order to design and drive the change and innovation processes. For each tool described, I will in the following describe an exercise, which a change process leader can use to strengthen his/her competence in handling this change process tool in the actual situation he or she is in.

First, however, I will describe the critical points for change process leaders as process owners and then the tools to be used to make the change process work.

1. Critical points for creating change

Based on my experience of 30 years of leadership and consulting in organizational change processes in many different kinds of organizations in various countries, I have reached the conclusion that there are three different levels of activity which horizontal change process leaders should concentrate on for the change process to be successful. At the same time, there are also three "leadership key activities" which should be applied in the change process. I will first put these items in a "3 by 3" matrix and then briefly characterize them.

I will concentrate on the items in a different way of change processing, so that leaders can more easily adopt them to implement change.

Change frame

Levels of activity	Leadership activities	1.2.1 Vision development	1.2.2 Networking	1.2.3 System development
1.1.1 Creating new organizational conditions				
1.1.2 Creating a new way of working and different behavior		**1.3 CHANGE PROCESS OWNERS**		
1.1.3 Creating a new work process with different steps				

1.1. Levels of activity

Creating new organizational conditions

In one project in a German Sparkasse bank, the chairman of the board was picturing a future situation, in which a sales person in the branch office would approach the customer in a more systematic way to help him profitably manage his money (stream) (for both parties). In reality, however, the customer representative in the front office was drinking coffee with customers, chatting about their families, but otherwise only passively reacting to the customer's requests, within the Sparkassen conditions.

For years, the chairman had been attempting to change all kinds of conditions in the organization to bring this customer representative in the front office to the business approach he had had in mind for so long. The computer systems were revamped, the building refurbished, customer representatives had been assigned their specific customer segments. New products were developed, greater flexibility for the sales staff was permitted, new systems, new working procedures, new salary schemes, etc. But the customer representative was still drinking coffee with customers and responding to their wishes. The staff introduced new client strategies, market analyses, support systems, etc. The customer representative was still drinking coffee, etc. This really got the chairman quite desperate. What else was he to do to facilitate change in the front? It became clear to him that he could continue to change conditions—but this did not necessarily change behavior. It required an investment at a deeper level.

Creating a new way of working and different behavior

One had to take a good look at the way the customer representatives were working with customers. Each customer representative had developed his individual way of working. There was a great variety in approaches to the customer. Some of them felt uncomfortable calling up customers and inviting them to discuss a new offer, others had a very quick but improvised way of responding to customers, and again others liked to impress their customers with computer data. It was not enough to send sales staff to training courses to learn new sales methods or different social behavior. What was required was a deeper understanding by the manager of the customer representative concerning the sales concept practiced by his co-worker. A new way of developing client strategies, trying a new way of approaching customers by telephone, a new way of preparing, having and evaluating client conversations, cross-selling techniques, these activities had to be acquired by practicing them under the guidance of a coach in actual work situations. This systematic action learning approach to get to a different way of working, to get a new systematic client approach in sales, to reach a different behavior, needed a long-term experimental process in which superiors and teams—with the help of external experts—developed their new ways of working with the customer.

Creating a new work process with different steps

This second layer of change immediately required a deeper look at the third layer of change: that is the redesign of the sales process as a total customer process. When examining the process of interacting with the customer in more detail, one is astonished of the complexity of this process in its entirety and the many steps that have to be taken to get towards the final result. Administrative procedures, checks and double checks, data gathering, decision making, make the process a non-transparent process. With the help of expert systems, many of these steps and complexities can be streamlined to help the salesmen facing the customer handle the whole process without any complicated process interfaces. This reduces working and writing time and limits the duration of the process.

1.2. Leadership activity

To be able to tackle these three levels of change, leaders need a different way of approaching the change issue than normally done within the operational structures, systems and procedures. These three levels of change are more easily accessible when the change process is led in a process way. This means that the process leader(s) need to adopt three key leadership activities to influence the change process.

Vision development

Leaders must develop a new vision for the required change. This vision should not only contain a view of the situation after the successful completion of the change process, but also include the key policies, by which this change process is going to be guided. If leadership is not willing to apply new or at least reviewed policies, if they do not communicate these new goals and policies, if they do not interact in this respect with the stakeholders, the change will end up getting bogged down and dying in the existing old patterns of behavior, thinking and working.

Networking

Leaders need to create and mobilize new networks of people to work on the change processes and they should assign specific roles in the process. Process owners, experts, customers, decision makers, legal authorities, and all those playing a specific role in the process must be energized, empowered and authorized to join the network as well. It is through these new networks of people that new ideas find their way into the organization and new interactions on these ideas can come alive.

System development

Existing systems often block changes from taking place. Change processes require new systems. These systems come into existence by experimenting with them and piloting on a small scale. Systems can be developed by using technological innovations and by new concepts of systems, based on the results from a learning process of initiative-takers and inventors.

1.3. Change process owners

The matrix picture shows the interdependence between layers of change and the activities of change leadership. On the one hand, change means that vision, networks and systems evolve independently to a new level through transforming conditions, behavior and process steps in a "learning by doing" process. On the other hand, conditions, behavior and process steps are created in a new way through vision, network and new system leadership interventions.

The two axes of the matrix are held together by the work of change process owners, and here we come to a key notion of change leadership, the central heart of the whole matter, *the* key issue of change: Who are the people who have the personality, the competence, the experience, the courage and the confidence to carry a change process through the full cycle from start to finish and into reality? Who are the key persons in the organization who have the power and strength to bring the change about? Who are the horizontal leaders?

The process owners as change process leaders are the key persons in leading the change process. They work on the basis of their own knowledge of the organization, their sense for the change issue they have to deal with, their intuitions for the next steps and how to deal with the people they interact with. But they also need some tools they can use to face the complexity of the situation and to give the process a sensible direction, to amplify the process and to do this in a conscious manner.

2. Tools for change

The tools, which I will be describing here, have been tested and proven by change process leaders as process owners when handling the complexities of the change process. Certain activities in the change process require a specific tool to support the progress. I will be introducing these tools as prompts, which might lead to working in a systematic way. I have also added some exercises for each tool to help horizontal leaders to strengthen their abilities in leading the process.

Tools
Change questions and questioning the change
Networking and relation building
Client connected aims and objectives
Policies that work as hidden directors
Building a vision of future and core values
Role responsibility
Handling time and designing process
Using resources

Tool 1: Changing questions and questioning the change

The ownership of a question

Questions are an expression of a need for change in reality. Questions need owners who can take care of this process of change.

"Who owns this question or issue?" is a marvellous statement the leader can make to keep situations transparent and clear. If there is no owner, it is difficult to do something substantial about the question.

If, on the other hand, there *is* an owner of the question, the change process can be consciously developed and completed.

The question as an expression of reality

Questions can be expressed in many different ways. In my experience there are three kinds of manifestations of a question.

- In the *maintenance question* the main focus is: "How can we improve the situation?"
- In the *problem question* the main focus is: "How can we find a solution to the problem?"
- In the *change question* the main focus is: "How can we find a new answer to the question?"

Each issue can be addressed at one of the three levels, and consequently there are three different kinds of responding processes, which will generate the answer to the question.

These three different processes are:

- The *maintenance process* that is reacting to an issue by adapting to the circumstances.
- The *problem-solving process* that is the research leading to the correct response.
- The *change process* that will transform the organization and the development of people.

It is crucial for the leadership to decide at which level the question or issue will be articulated and with which kind of process we should respond to it.

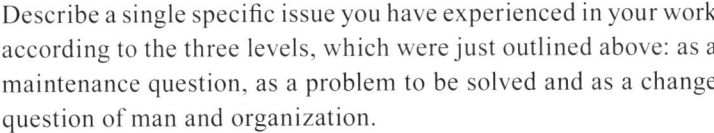

Exercise 1: Formulate the issue

Describe a single specific issue you have experienced in your work according to the three levels, which were just outlined above: as a maintenance question, as a problem to be solved and as a change question of man and organization.

Which process appears to be the most appropriate response to the question and why?

Example:
- "Our managers need an update on the latest management sales tools," *maintenance level.*
- "Our managers need to improve their techniques on how to solve complex problems in their team," *problem solving level.*
- "Our managers were invited to explore new ways of dealing with complex matters," *change level.*

Questioning
Working with questions requires the ability to pose the correct questions.

93

Questions can be asked with two different kinds of aims in mind:

To gather information for *oneself* and to understand the content of the issue better, or to start an engagement, which might help *the other person* to express what the issue is.

The first aim is more oriented towards the past; the second more towards the future.

However, whilst clarifying an issue for oneself is the more appropriate method in the maintenance and problem solving process, posing questions to others is *tapping* into wider resources— and as a consequence, the leader as a manager has to come up with possible solutions and actions to take. The leader/manager is expected to be in control, which is appropriate in the operational context where the work process is done.

The second type of questioning fits the process of change more. There is a need to investigate in more depth and with an open attitude of the leader, through questioning, the situation and events that happen, in order to start to understand what is going on, and only then can the next step in the process be found. The owner of the question is aided by the questioning, to reflect on this and also to discover different opportunities and ways of dealing with the issue.

By asking the right questions, the other person is helped to analyze the actual situation, and in rephrasing the issue one sees new opportunities for action.

Exercise 2: Questioning in two ways

In relation to a real issue in the work situation:

1. question another person to understand the issue and then come up with solutions, and then
2. help the other person to describe the issue better and define the next step of this process.

Note the difference in how this works for the other person and for yourself.

Tool 2: Networking and relationship building

To be able to lead and create change, you have to connect to other persons. Networking is a key process for leadership. Changing and developing the organization works by creating networks that in turn explore opportunities and take further initiatives. This is indeed very important in the context of change.

In the operational context, the networks are more or less in place, being related to someone's function and role. In the change context, however, you have to find the right networks and create them to make them work in the interest of the change issue.

Exercise: Evaluate and create your change networks

Put yourself in the center of a circle and place the key people around you, whom you are working with on the key change issue.

Characterize the type of relationship you have with each person.

Is the relation dominated by the formal connection you have with the other person, because of the function and position of that person in the hierarchical organization in comparison to your own function and position?

Is the relationship dominated by the role of being experts and having expertise that you share with the other person?

Is the relationship dominated by an entrepreneurial and initiative-taking link you might have with the other person?

Do you want to change the connection with the other since this relationship is not so relevant anymore in your change process, or—quite the opposite—do you intend to invest more into this relationship?

What is the key step you have to undertake to make this change happen?

Tool 3: Client-connected aims and objectives

Target group awareness

In the process of creating change it is essential for the leadership to remain aware of the fact that it needs to make sense for the customer. It is the customer who will ultimately validate and accept the change of a product or service for their own process. Being aware of the customer process and engaging with him on his requirements for change will guide you to find out what it is the customer needs and what you need to do next.

Exercise 1: The link to the customer and product use

Who are the people you work for, the customer requiring your product or service in their life or work situation?

What are they doing with these products or services? What does it mean to them? Is it essential in their process or is it just a "nice-to-have"? Do they have a need for change and have they expressed it?

Imagining results

Setting specific targets for a change can be an abstract activity. Targets only work for people when they are tangible and distinct and can be visualized as orientation points for their change process. Others will also be imagining the future result of what they want to achieve. It is helpful to be transparent about the images you have to the others, certainly in leadership, and analyze differences in these images with the other people involved in the change process.

Exercise 2: Picturing the future

What is your image of the future as a result from a change process, where do you think you need to arrive? Is this picture shared by others or do they have a different view?

Share these possibly differing images!

Definition of aims and objectives
To define a target in the change process, it is essential to be concrete.

To do so, one can use the following four elements in the definition of the target.

1. Define the desired future behavior and/or activity as precisely as possible.
2. Make the target measurable by the definition of a standard or norm.
3. Decide on a time frame in which the target will have to be achieved.
4. Be precise about the resources required for reaching the target.

An example: "We envisage that within two years, 80% of our customers will be drinking our new product twice a day at home and at work."

Another example: "In half a year, our typical employee beyond the age of 45 has put one personal idea for improvement in his/her work situation or work process into practice."

Exercise 3: Target/issue definition

Try to define as precisely as possible your targets/issues for change in your area of responsibility in your organization.

Working with scenarios
In the process of target setting for change it is often a good idea to work with scenarios. Scenarios are images of future situations which might come true. You could construct different scenarios for the same situation, like a stability scenario, a change scenario and an improvement scenario. In building scenarios one can use different elements, for instance:

*   extrapolation of trends and facts,
*   predictions in the future by experts and specialists,
*   signals and indications given by customers,
*   your own dreams you have about the future.

Exercise 4: Building scenarios

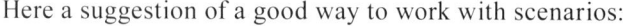

Here a suggestion of a good way to work with scenarios:

You make three different but plausible pictures of how the future situation could look like concerning the development of your company, department, team or function. The different scenarios must all be based on real variations, not three simple deviations from the same situation.

To build the scenarios, you will need to describe:
- how the future situation will be,
- what the actual change was,
- the future behavior of the relevant people,
- the factors and developments which influenced the situation,
- the policies which are at work in the way the situation is handled.

However, after having built the three scenarios you should not immediately dive into working towards one of three. You should rather ask yourself the question: If I look at all three scenarios, which decision should I take or what is my highest priority? And consequently: What then could my first irreversible step be? As you can never predict the future precisely, scenarios can help you to be better prepared for future situations you create through the entrepreneurial crafting of your own future.

Tool 4: Policies that work as hidden directors

To implement change, one needs to be aware of the policies guiding the behavior of the people involved in the change process.

One can often see differences between policies on paper and actually implemented policies. To become aware of your policies, you can look at the policies at work and you can look at the policies you would like to use as a leader to guide the change process into the future.

Exercise: Done policies

To understand the actually implemented policies, you will have to analyze the real situation and behavior. Through this you then will discover the leading principles directing and driving behavior.

- Describe to other people the actual situation in which there was a need for change to become visible.
- Describe the actual space or room people were in.
- Describe the moment in time when it occurred.
- Describe what was said by people in that situation.
- Describe your own feelings and emotions in that situation.

The result of this description should be like showing a video taken of the real-life situation.

When a clear picture has emerged, you can try to characterize this picture together with the other stakeholders. This is not the idea to pass a judgment on the situation, but it is about telling the others what you find striking—and hence decisive—in the description.

After this characterization you can try to define the active policy, the driving principles steering the behavior of a person in that very situation. The identification of this actual policy can be seen as the discovery of "the hidden director" in the situation.

To give an example

The situation demanding a change is: You are together with another peer in your manager's office and you are jointly discussing a customer's complaint. You say: "I had this customer on the telephone and she said, 'This is the last time I will accept your excuse for a delayed delivery. If it happens once more, you will have lost our custom.'" You ask the others, "What can we to do about this?"

Your manager says, "Don't get nervous. I have had this problem with this same customer before. They can't leave us; they have no other suppliers to turn to."

And your colleague then says, "Sorry, but it is making me nervous, because this is not the only customer with this type of complaint."

The characterization could be:
- There is an angry customer, who will not accept another single delay for a delivery.
- The manager reacts passively by recounting past experiences with this customer and plays it down.
- The colleague shows that—as this is not the only case of a complaint for delayed delivery—there might be a more significant and fundamental issue to address.

What are the hidden directors?

The situation shows the confrontation between two different hidden directors:
- You and your colleague: when a customer wants to abandon the business relation ship, we have to act immediately and improve our performance.
- The manager: when the customer has no alternative, she is not a priority.

New policies

Change is needed when there is a fundamental difference in steering convictions between the key people involved in the process. The difference in this situation and the need for (change) action will also be applicable in many other situations. The leadership has to see to it that the "hidden directors" are evident and that we move ourselves to more common ground, balancing the customer's, employee's and superior's steering convictions.

Creating and implementing change is not in the least about the creation of new policies or steering convictions to act out of.

To create new and shared steering policies, it is first of all necessary to have a shared awareness of what the new steering policy could be.

As shown above, the first step is "policy identification". In policy identification, you try to describe the principles, values and norms you want to see directing the future behavior of all people involved.

To postulate new policies, you have to:
• be concrete and precise,
• keep it simple,
• keep it achievable.

It is important that everyone required to integrate the new policy into their future behavior is also involved in the process of policy development.

A second step is to create little experiments in which the new policy is acted out. By trying it out and testing the results, one discovers the necessary abilities and competencies corresponding with the new policy. It is a learning process, in which concrete experiences are being evaluated. Monitoring as to what extent this new behavior leads to the desired results is important because the whole process is interactive and also influenced by "outsiders", who are not directly involved.

Based on these experimental results, one can come to a policy decision in a third step.

This means that the new policy becomes formalized and will be the normal policy in the future, to which everyone involved will be required to adhere to. Policy decision making is not something that can be done behind closed doors. It is a process in which people involved in the process respond in a different way to the recent past. This creates new realities in organizations.

Tool 5: Building a vision of future and core values

Building a vision is an essential act of leadership in the change process. To create change, it is necessary to develop a real-life vision of the future of the business you are in. By building a vision you add "sense" as ingredient to the change process.

The leadership's vision of the change is a mental expression of the core values of the company.

Exercise: Core vision

Ask yourself this question:
- What is it we are really good at?
- What is it the customer really values in our product or service?
    The vision can and should be based on the answers to these questions.

Change strategy
Building a vision is essential for the change strategy.
    The change strategy has two dimensions:
- the way we change our business,
- the way we change our organization.

It does not make any sense to simply have a change planning process in the company. However, this makes more sense when the leadership sets up a cycle in which the key people on different levels in the community engage in a horizontal way about the future. The ensuing dialogue is based on observations and intentions of the people involved. It will also be tested in the light of trends and messages from outside the company.

    Change strategy building can best be described as a process in which there is *forecasting—monitoring—evaluating*.

    In the *forecasting* we try to project what might happen and how we would react.

    In the *monitoring* we track the actual activities and document the surprises, when the results differ from our expectations.

In the *evaluation* we draw our conclusions, try to learn and become aware of the blind spots we appear to have had.

This process forms the basis for the organizational development process, in which we translate the strategy into more specific parameters to measure the effects.

Tool 6: Role responsibility

Responsibilities are primarily connected to the role one performs in the change process. The roles require adequate competencies. In the change process it is not about functional competencies, but it is about personal competencies.

In the change process there is a constant need to clarify the responsibilities. "Who is responsible for what?"

Exercise: Responsibilities

To help identify your specific responsibilities in the change process role, you can ask yourself three questions:
- What is your role and for which results are you accountable?
- What personal competencies do you have to show in the change process?
- What are the initiatives you need to take to make the process work?

To investigate the *value* of your role, you might ask the following questions:
- What would happen if my role would disappear?
- What would happen if I would leave the change process?

Tool 7: Handling time and designing process

In the change process the time management is crucial.

There is a simple formula concerning handling of time:

Time = availability = priority = personal policy.

Everyone has 24 hours to a day. That is a simple fact. But time has also a subjective element. Some people have lots of time, whilst others are always short of it. To handle one's time is to handle one's availability. To whom will I make myself available is a key decision in the change process. To choose to be available is practically the same as setting your priority. Priorities are not automatically the first points on a long list; they are the choices I make of whom to be available to.

To be fully accessible, present and committed is essential to the quality of the change process. If you are physically there, but your heart is not in it or your mind is elsewhere, then there is a lack of quality in the change process.

To be able to choose to be there, you need a personal policy to guide you. If your personal policy is that "work always comes first," the change process will suffer. The personal policy for steering your time allocation is a balancing policy between different interests. The first step is to become consciously aware of your present policy of the way you handle your availability for the change process, and see whether this leads to satisfactory results. To do so, you should analyze your pattern, as shown in the following exercise.

Exercise 1: Analyze a day

From the moment you wake up till the moment you go to sleep, what does your day look like? Can you discover any special pattern in your day? Can you distinguish between work phases and a non-work phases?

Different jobs have different time patterns. The question can be: Are you available for the important things in the change process, or are you being pushed around by the urgent demands of the day-to-day operations?

Exercise 2: Analyze a week

You can visualize your pattern:

	Morning	Afternoon	Evening	Night
Monday				
Tuesday				
Wednesday				
Thursday				
Friday				
Saturday				
Sunday				

Can you discover the pattern of your working week? You move through the week in a certain way. When are your operational management meetings, when do you visit customers, when are you involved in the change process?

If you discover a pattern, you can ask yourself whether this pattern answers the requirements of what you really want to do. Is it possible to change the pattern and can you engage with others, who also depend on your time pattern, about it?

It might be that you want to be available for everybody all the time. This can easily ruin your week to begin with! You have to explore and decide on a good policy in handling your priorities throughout the week. Try to experiment with little changes in your time pattern before you change the basic pattern more radically.

Exercise 3: Analyze a month

There will also be monthly rhythms in your pattern: certain meetings or visits follow a monthly agenda. If you can identify this rhythm, you are better equipped to prepare yourself in advance. Some people are always too late and they live under constant pressure. To be able to relax a bit more, it is valuable to be a little ahead of time.

These rhythms also reflect your responsibilities and the responsibilities of others. Concentrate on your own responsibilities and do not interfere too much with the responsibilities of others.

Exercise 4: Analyze a year

It is good to reflect at the end of the year. What did you do during the year, and was it in line with what you actually wanted to do? What did you learn? Look ahead into the next year. How have you arranged your agenda, and how is your annual rhythm in terms of work, holiday and other life situations? Is it well balanced?

Make the day, week, month and year pattern visible to yourself. Discover the friction points, the moments that offer only little added value. Can you design different patterns and experiment with them? Look at the processes you are in and that run parallel in your life. Do you have a process awareness, do you spend the right amount of time and energy on them?

Tool 8: Using resources

Money

Money is part of the change process when the implementation actually commences. It is a good thing to closely monitor the way you handle money in the change process. There is incoming and outgoing money. Are they in balance? Is money spent on things you value for the future, or is it spent on old obligations from the past?

Exercise: Monitoring money streams

Draw up an overview of the incoming and outgoing money streams in the course of the change process.

- Which sources generated the incoming money?
- What was the money spent on?
- Where do you see an imbalance between incoming and outgoing money?
- Can you identify what you have to change to balance these streams?

It is an interesting exercise to track the change process as if it would be an independent company.

- You can analyze the invoices you received and paid.
- Can you envision who the people behind the bills are? Who is on the receiving end, who is the sender?
- How are these people contributing, what was the activity generating this invoice?
- Is there something you want to change in this?

However, when it comes to "change", it is often not only about tools but sometimes even more about emotions.

A leadership experience:
The hospital director

A few years ago, two hospitals were merged and now represent one single organization, headed by one general director. He formed a management team composed of two healthcare managers, one facility manager, one head of human resources and one head of finances. Two senior doctors, acting as coordinators for the medical staff, are also part of the management team.

The cooperation in the management team is leaving a lot to be desired, as there is a rift between two different parties: the medical side (the doctors) versus the business (represented by the administrative managers). Taking decisions in this management team is not all that easy, because both interest groups in the organization have to be involved in the process. After working in this constellation for some time, the members of the management team are at loggerheads; employees start to complain about a lack of transparency in their management's decisions.

The general director decides to organize a few special "away days" for the management team to dialogue as a group about the pending problems. They conclude that each member of the management team also should care for a company-wide policy issue, besides his principal functional responsibility. However, this creates even more problems in the team. The division of power and the lack of a transparent structure and decision making block any sensible resolution to the problem.

Finally, the general director decides to step in with a drastic measure, by changing the internal structure of the hospital. He regroups the hospital's departments and teams into new units. The segmentation of the groups is determined by the consistent type of patient (and their sickness), each new unit being allocated their own budgets and funds, staff and team structure. Every unit is managed by a two-person team, consisting of one administrative and one medical manager. This new leadership structure is now flexible enough to take the necessary decisions within the agreed framework. The management team needs to coach these new managers and to take responsibility for the overall processes of the hospital.

The financial manager becomes the hospital's controller. The facility manager takes care of all the supporting service processes. All staff departments are integrated into one single unit.

This substantial structural change obviously affects the medical staff, the work council and the supervisory board. They have to take up a position concerning this drastic change. Three of the leading doctors resist the change strongly, but see themselves outrun by the events as they start to lose their influence after a while.

The newly appointed administrative business managers are supported in their new role by going through a coaching and learning process together. They train in the key qualities of horizontal leadership, which are involved when designing a process, coaching people in their learning, developing and communicating visions and moving an organization by their bold decisions. The medical managers, too, are trained in the basics of management and how to interact with their colleague doctors in a positive and constructive way.

The hospital director:

"I want the responsibility delegated all the way through the organization and stopping at the specific people, who are close to the client process and can thus be seen as responsible and able to act. I was getting very tired of the overly complex decision making processes. Everybody was hiding behind somebody else. Now we can steer the organization in a much more practical and direct way. We have successfully installed a simpler budget procedure, the managers know what they can influence and what not. We have installed company-wide forums where the top management can deal with others on company-wide issues. Each forum is headed by a top management member. This person can then take a decision after consulting those who are actually involved. I myself now act as the board of directors. I am now able to focus on the next steps in the development of the hospital as a whole. We have to look into the financial streams and cut costs; but I also see the next merger already appearing on the horizon. Now that we have implemented a clear structure and clear responsibilities, the managers themselves can concentrate on improving the work processes and the quality of our health-care activities. I see very fast progress in these issues today."

PART TWO

In part two, I will now move on to explore the leadership methodology, which is about implementing change and development in organizations. It is based on the research of real cases in organizations where change and development processes took place. These cases have been reviewed and interpreted, and out of it came viewpoints, which might be useful as handrails in the arranging processes of change and development. We have especially researched the role of horizontal leadership and came to some surprising conclusions. This methodology and approach is being applied in real-life practice, as it is related to the views of leaders and other people involved with the basic values of mankind and the images of man one is thinking and acting with. We will see the individual as the one who is able to create change and development out of his free will. We will explore fundamental images of man and organizations and social development based on this premise.

A leadership experience:
The non-profit organization—
the need for leadership

The director of a non-profit organization invited me to have a look at his organization, which was indeed facing some trouble. He was looking for the next development step to move the organization toward better grounds, but wanted someone to look with him and be a sounding board in this process.

After having talked with various people in the organization, I gave him my impression:

"In the past, this organization was paying more attention to the great opportunities and contributions in society and very much less to what this meant to the people inside the organization. The internal substance had been worn down and people did not have sufficient energy and stamina to face the ever-increasing demands of the outside world. What is needed now is to spend more time on the immanent issues this community is facing and to approach the subject in a systematic way.

Many good colleagues have left the organization, many are sick and not able to return and the ones still here are not really happy. Newcomers drop out again after a relative short period because they are disappointed: disappointed in that their ideals are not transformed into reality, but that they are rather met by the shortcomings of this organization.

There is a culture of trying to keep the ideals at a high level; but the most important external partners and financiers are not taken seriously, and rather than to actually demonstrate the success of the organization, these stakeholders are only asked to 'believe' in impressive propaganda stories relayed to them. The number of members in the organization is stagnating, at best, if not dwindling. There has been no progress of the public image, and during the last seven years there was no new review of the organization's mission and how this mission was to be put into practice.

This situation requires a systematic process of development and change, done in a consistent way, touching upon the essentials of the organization. It should be enacted with all present staff members still willing to move the organization forward in a well-led process.

Clarifying the issues, identifying means and processes to tackle them, mobilizing the staff and the partners in the development process would need to be the first step."

The four issues

The director introduced an organizational development process. He identified four issues and selected process owners to take them on and get them resolved.

The *first* issue was the **balance of two parts** of the organization, both in importance and power: the one department handling the social projects and the other the fund-raising department.

The *second* issue was the **improvement of the well-being** of the employees and their identification with the targets of the organization.

The *third* issue was the **revitalization and improvement of the external relations**.

The *fourth* issue was the **review of both mission and vision** and finding the strategy for the future.

At first, the process owners started by engaging colleagues and important external partners and stakeholders, asking them to participate in the process and to bring their ideas to the table. This very quickly resulted in research and some experimental steps with these ideas. In a reiterative rhythm, the director and the process owners discussed the progress in the processes, the bottlenecks and blockers that were met, and the next steps.

It turned out that the work processes in the different parts of the organization were complex and unclear. A lot of effort was invested in clarifying these processes, simplifying them again and identifying the correct person to be in charge of this work process to be performed and completed properly.

The second step was to understand how important the cooperation between idealistic specialists is to get to the targeted results. It is simply not enough when everybody is only busy with their own "babies". Projects will only turn out successfully when there is a sufficient degree of exchange between colleagues and external partners. A lot of energy and attention was given to acquire the respectively needed skills for good cooperation and good project management.

Views of the people involved
During the development process, almost all the people involved were asked for their views on the process and what could be improved. Here some of their remarks:

> *"I was happy to be asked to contribute and felt good about the enthusiasm of some colleagues. They really got me going."*

"I was satisfied with the observation that we allowed for some time to really talk about the problems."

"It made a lot of sense to have a look into the work processes of the others—but I did have difficulty in managing my own priorities during the process."

"We were able to make a complex new project work. Without our new organizational development process, it would never have been possible. It was a bit hard, however, to see some colleagues leave."

"It was essential that we clearly communicated the steps and results and kept each other in the loop of information."

"In this organizational development process, we created a different way of working together. We were able to overcome the (mental) islands and many good fruits came out of this."

"It was funny to see how many problems we thought we had disappeared when we actually started on the real issues."

"The process looks slow and cumbersome, but that is o.k. for this kind of work."

"In the beginning, I found the chaos difficult to handle. So many processes to address simultaneously! At some point, though, it all came together and became more simple again. Now we have to look at our structure and change it in order to be able to continue on a more structural scale."

A new structure

It soon became clear that the internal structure of this organization was blocking the work processes. The organization was divided into two major departments, each with a departmental head, and in each department a group of specialists was working on their individual issues, without any regard to the issues outside their own department. This aspect was taken up by the director. He regrouped the whole organization into a number of different teams, giving each team their own team leader. These team leaders were picked on the base of the skills they had displayed in the change and development process and their competence in the field they were working in.

The teams were then set to the task of identifying their customers, defining their budget as well as planning for improvements in the professionalism and the quality of cooperation between the team members. The team leaders were coached by the two new department heads, who meanwhile had been selected by the director. Together they formed the management team. This team started an organization-wide process of reviewing the mission and vision statements. They also spent a lot of time communicating to the outside partners about the internal activities and measures taken to improve the situation.

The need for leadership

A non-profit organization, with a world-wide presence and frequently being confronted with complex and sensitive (sometimes political) issues and problems, will often be exposed and put in a vulnerable position. Why?

First of all, because this kind of organization attracts idealistic people dreaming of a better world, but with difficulties linking that dream with reality and finding the way to "make it happen". There is a great danger of getting frustrated by the little progress that is made and a hostile outside world that does not understand what is needed and what should be done. In this kind of setting, expectations and pressure laid on one another are considerable. You have to consistently meet high standards over a long period of time. The process continually requires new initiatives, a great sense of personal responsibility and engagement, the desire to cooperate and to help one another. Funding is by no means secure, there often is little recompensation in the form of recognition compared to the sacrifices people have to make. And then there is the complex network of relations with many different parties that have their own options and preferences. This truly requires a strong leadership that can act and lead horizontally and is capable of bringing the community together on the path of systematic development and change without losing touch with its roots.

CHAPTER 6: # The horizontal leadership research—three case stories

1. Introduction

Over the past years, we developed three hypotheses, based on our experience and systematic research of the horizontal leadership theme in connection to organizational development processes.

The first hypothesis is that all the personal issues, questions, intentions and desires of top managers will very much destine and decide on the development of others in the organization. If top management is enthusiastic to explore a certain issue, then people in the organization will be given room to explore this certain subject. If we want to create space for certain issues, themes or subjects in an organization, then top management must themselves open up and be prepared to move forward. This is one of the first challenges for developmental leadership.

The second hypothesis is that middle management, which is strongly embedded in the hierarchical power structure, plays a central and decisive role in the change and development processes and thus in the leadership process. To the extent that middle management opens up more to the horizontal space, exploring and experimenting with their teams on change and development, the organization will be better able to tackle these change issues. The execution of the key qualities of horizontal leadership, as indicated before, plays a crucial role in working on the change issues.

The third hypothesis is that, if the change process is dealing with issues which involve processes with the customer and his interests and is not only concentrating on internal organizational issues, the change process will have more impact and the organization will gain in future potential.

When these three hypotheses are explored in more depth in the organization, the people in the organization have a higher level of sensitivity on the pending change issues. As a result, the organization will prosper more and will be able to face its challenges better. This does not mean that this organization will not also have to solve problems and that everything only runs smoothly. But in this organization the community of people involved will be better equipped and prepared to perform the two processes—the operational work process and the change process—and at the same time integrate the results of the change processes into their operational work process.

We have been researching these hypotheses ourselves over the last seven years in more then 20 organizations in different countries in different parts of the world. We have been using the following method of research and experimentation.

2. Method of research and experimentation

In an exploring dialogue with the top management of an organization, we share the approach to be applied and how it can be performed in this organization. The people involved in the research process are selected, the customer processes in which the observations can be made are identified, and there is a general agreement on how everyone in the process will jointly share their experiences and findings; this method automatically leads to identifying the next development steps in the organization.

In separate engagements with top managers, their individual drives and motives are explored. What keeps these persons (inwardly) busy, what are their commitments demonstrated in the ongoing development and change processes? They, then, as top managers share with each other the way they execute their leadership within and outside the organization, and how they think this is received and seen in the organization.

Then there are the engagement sessions with middle managers, in which there is a common analysis of how they get involved themselves in the change processes and how well they explore the horizontal space. Also, they are asked to respond to a questionnaire with 16 questions concerning the four key qualities of horizontal leadership in a 360° analysis (see attachment page 186). The line manager, two peers and four co-workers also are invited to answer the leadership questionnaire and then share their views with the middle manager on how the horizontal leadership qualities of this leader are externally perceived by others. The middle manager then does the analysis on the results from the 360° analysis and shares the gained insights with the others who were involved in this leadership research process. Differences in scores are explored and discussed, and the person can draw conclusions from this. All middle managers involved in the research process share their experiences and insights in a conference and thus discover important issues and themes, concerning the organization and the way it develops. It becomes clear and evident how the issues are handled and the critical factors for success are identified.

A key step in the research process is to make sure that sufficient opportunities are created to make observations and to reflect with customers on what the issues and themes are in the customer process. The customer interfaces playing a role in the day-to-day operations and being expressed by the customer as being important for him in the relationship with this organization. It is here that it becomes visible how the customer process and organizational process match—or do not match.

After having taken these steps, the question is explored as to what the findings in these three lines of research—that of the top management, the middle management and the employee/customer relationship—have in common or not. Is there any link to be found between the phenomena and the questions of these three different strands of research? This is also the theme for the final meeting—with the consultant—where everybody involved in the process is present. Now, the next development step of the organization will become clearer. This leads to a further process of reflection, investigation and experimentation.

To illustrate how this research approach was done in the practice, I will now describe three cases we selected from the many cases explored during the past years.

Case story 1: The trade union

The director of a Dutch trade union observes a number of issues in his organization: a decline in membership numbers, an increasing demand from the members for improved services to the individual well-being question, the absence of a clear union position concerning some hot issues in the Dutch society, and the lack of collective activities. The mission of this trade union is in jeopardy and its future is at stake. Over the last few years, there was too little progress in creating a broader foundation for the organization's future, despite it having a strong and meaningful past.

The chairman starts discussing with his colleagues on the board, with middle management and co-workers, with members and external parties. These meetings create the insight needed for a different kind of approach to the development process. The process is launched and based on a different guiding principle than the previous one, which had been in place for decades.

Backed by his own observations but also by scientific research from others, he creates the image that socially innovative companies are more successful than others. He regards this assumption a good starting point for the next step. The "raison d'être" of the labor unions is to tend to the collective interests of the workers, their members, and when necessary they will protect these interests with the classical methods, such as strikes and confrontation. In day-to-day practice, however, the members have many more individual interests they want to see being met by the labor union. For instance, they would like to be offered the service of completing the yearly tax form for them.

Reflection on values

The director of the union concludes that the labor union must go through an intense phase of reflection on its values. "We want to be value-driven," and "concentrate on the issue of not excluding people, but rather including them in the process of developing our union," is the director's position. There is a need for a new type of solidarity "beyond the fat I," as the humanistic Professor Harry Kunneman tends to call this. It might be even "beyond the fat we", the selfish optimizing of only our own interests at the expense of others.

The management of this union is being challenged to take up this issue with the organization. However, due to some financial imbalance in the union, the director decides to first restructure the union to simplify matters and have a better match between income and costs. As a result, middle management is going through some hard times. Some of them resist the initiative; but there are a few who are enthusiastic about this new step. For over one year, there is a continuous process of meetings and engagement sessions on this subject, first in small circles, then in the whole community. Research is done, seminars and conferences are organized, and new brochures are published with vision and mission statements. The director and the office manager spend a lot of time in dialogues with others to stimulate the process of change and development. The regional centers of the union show the highest resistance levels. The union representatives want to hold on to the old values and ways of working. They relate strongly with the basic ideological guiding principles, which had worked well for so many years. They feel a personal commitment towards these. This is actively taken up by the director, who in regular visits discusses this issue and attempts to understand the differences of vision and the guiding principles in the union and deal with them.

The research process

In the context of the leadership research process, the director decides to introduce an external researcher, who uses the described approach to intensify the dialogue on the key issues in the community. There are engagement sessions with the top and middle management, company union representatives and co-workers in the offices. The research is now centered on the work processes, how they are being appreciated by the customer, what successes and failures are being experienced; whether there is a biographical connection between the people and the organization, and how they deal with these issues. With the help of the 360° questionnaire on horizontal leadership, the middle management reflects on the way they act out the key horizontal leadership qualities and how they actually are making use of the horizontal space. It becomes clear that internally most people are aware of the new direction the union should be moving to. They are in the process of linking into this movement and curious of how this will become evident in their work process. There is a common process, but there is also one sensitive and difficult spot: the staff representatives in the associated companies, where the members of the union are employed, are not systematically involved in this process; hence, they are not aware of it. The staff representatives have to deal with the members in the different companies and communicate the new vision and mission to them. However, this fails. An intensified dialogue with these core members ensues, they are invited more systematically to participate in the change process and are coached to find their own viewpoint and communicate with the members on the key change issues.

The director:

"Leadership, customer process and social innovation need authentic people. Human beings actively participate in the community, and when they can be fully authentic there, they are able to offer the maximum contribution to the organization. That is why we talk to each other about the individual biography of our people, how their biography is connected to the biography of our organization, which values and norms are important to the individual, and can they see them being applied in the organization? Based on Christian social thinking, we have taken up the position that these are values helping us to build a better community. This, again, is the basis for an improved process with our customers. We have asked our organization the meaningful key question: If we would stop with the rou-

tine Monday morning meeting and, instead, would start discussing with colleagues what they would like to do and what not, which values they consider important, would that not improve the way we cooperate and get results together?

Another question we raised was about our knowledge of humanity. What do we know about human nature? Compare this knowledge to what we know about products, systems, et cetera. I have come to the conclusion that human resource management is a bag of tricks, which is used to make people work harder. We would do better to work on social innovation and care about what people really experience. The idea that values are our core, we now can practice more by concentrating on people and getting deeper insights about the other person. And if you are the leader, how can you love your customers and colleagues, when you are not doing just that and connecting with them?"

Top management leadership

Based on this experience, the director decides to invite six top managers from other companies for a special individual dialogue meeting on these issues of values, leadership, new solidarity and Sense-Making. How do top managers see this in relation to their own organizations? How do they act out the leadership and how do they involve the employees, customers and other stakeholders in the process of company development and change? In the course of this meeting, they discover how unusual this subject is for them in their daily business. They are very skilled in speaking in their well-known jargon about company growth and turnover, staff numbers, business issues and future strategies—but it is not so customary for them to talk about questions like Sense-Making, researching and experimenting of change issues, reflective engagement sessions with their organization, examining a connection between the organizational and the personal biography. However, as the dialogue warms up, they come to realize how useful these reflections are for their personal leadership and how it shows effects in their company. It is as if there were a hidden door to working life being opened, the inside world of the leaders becoming visible for a moment. It encourages the director of the union to continue with this process in his organization, it shows the future potential of having these dialogue meetings in the customer organizations. Finally, it can give the union's community a perspective on what its future mission could be. It will take a long time and will require many steps before the core members will have internalized these aspects of Sense-Making and leadership, which is, nevertheless, what the chairman expects to happen.

Case story 2: The national institute

In a national institute, with thousands of civil servants employed on governmental processes, one of the top managers concluded that the organization was not performing very well when having to react to negative newspaper reports on the institute. "Is there a lack of leadership?" he asked himself. He discussed this question with a number of his colleagues and in general meetings, where they all agreed that this was a serious issue, which should be addressed. "How is our leadership working?" was the central question they decided to research and develop.

In a further session, first- and second-line managers from different parts of the institute were invited in pairs to participate in a research process that would look into this question. Before the first meeting, each person examined, with the 360° questionnaire on horizontal leadership, the way he/she explored the horizontal space. Two leaders were invited for a series of meetings: one from inside the institute and one from outside. Both leaders gave a short personal introduction on how they act in leadership, and then discussed their individual position among each other, before finally entering into the general engagement with the whole group. The members of the group were then divided into syndicate groups, where they shared their personal ways of dealing with leadership and how they could connect their own way of leading with what had been said in the introductory contributions by the two invited leaders. After every session, each person could either work at home on a leadership issue they had selected or work with others in their own department or team. They were asked to write down their experiences and findings in a personal note and circulate it to the others. Through this process, a lot of intellectual and emotional exchange went on in the institute on this leadership issue in quite a short period of time.

Some quotes from participants:

"I do not like to use the word leadership. I prefer to use the word guidance of people. I think of the verse: pick the apples when they are ripe. Hear the question people are raising—that is, what it is all about! You have to practice really listening continuously. I'm also grateful for having been asked to participate in this process. It is important to work with surprises, to do things in a slightly different way. Otherwise you risk falling asleep. It is about the unusual und unconventional. It is also important to create a flow that involves the people. I do not know exactly how to do that in practice.

You certainly have to create a good atmosphere, connect with the people and take up a clear position at times."

"Our leadership is not exactly a shining example in personal communication. You have to learn to really listen to staff and try to make life easier for them. The vision must also be translated into the daily routines, so that the co-workers can understand why it is we do things in a certain way. For a long time, there was little attention paid to the human aspect in the organization: there must be more leadership, which works towards growing people, both professionally and personally at the same time."

"In our department I often hear that nobody is irreplaceable. In terms of quantity, this might be true: when somebody leaves, he will be replaced. In terms of quality and sense, however, making such remarks does not fully reflect reality. Everyone's contribution to the organization is unique; it is a result of how he or she stands in the organization and makes sense of the work they do. Being regarded as 'not to be missed', as a simple number, is neither good for the people or for the organization."

An experiment

One of the common findings of the reflective research and experimental process was that managers tend to only communicate on these issues at their own hierarchical level. Directors discuss it with directors, department heads with department heads, team leaders with team leaders, and workers with workers. In the process, the participants came to the surprising conclusion that the customer did not seem to play an important role. It was also shown that a dialogue going across different levels and specifically addressing customer issues was experienced as much more useful. This gave us the idea for another new experiment. Departments of the institute would form a team consisting of the director, a department head, two team leaders and two co-workers. More teams with a similar composition from other organizations were also invited to participate in the process. A half-year research and experimental process with three one-day meetings was organized; the teams would examine the change processes in their business, what worked well and what not, whilst the focus would be fully on the customer process in its interaction with the organizational processes.

The new experiment: Three meetings and a process

In the first one-day session, the change question is researched with the help of the five dimensions of our research methodology. I will be describing the five dimensions in more detail later in the book; however, for now let me briefly outline the process:

Each of the five dimensions is explored in a separate one-and-a-half-hour session in the following sequence:

1. Identify the change issue the team observes in their practical business.
2. Examine how this issue is being addressed in practice.
3. Has this issue played a role in the organization's past?
4. What are the personal biographical links of team members with this issue?
5. What are the guiding principles which determine how we handle the change question in practice?

Doing this in the above described particular constellation of the teams leads to an intensive and deepening dialogue among the team members. It is satisfying to see how the co-workers can contribute very actively in the process and how the higher levels, by their interested questioning and listening, open the space to free exchange of ideas.

After the first day, the team members return home, but they individually keep on dialoguing with many others in the organization on the issue the team has chosen. They discuss the issue in practice with others, and through this dialogue the issue becomes more known in the community.

After two months, the teams report back on their findings and learning experiences in the second meeting. Two teams interview each other in turn and give each other feedback and tips for their respective next steps. This helps the teams to find good testing grounds and methods for the next phase.

The results are then shared in the last common session. By sharing of findings and experiences, the issue is more widely disseminated in the organization and people in the community start to deal with it in a creative way. There is also a bridge built between the different hierarchical levels of the organization and a much better understanding about the differences in observation and interpretation on the different levels. There is a common interest in dealing with the development issues in a horizontal way.

The observed phenomena

We have experimented with ten teams in two half-year rounds and we discovered some interesting phenomena.

The dialogue within the team is intensive and deepening from the first minute. Although the participants are not familiar with the process, they are inwardly moved by it, there is space for a personal interaction among each other.

From the start, there is a common exploration of questions, issues and themes and how they work in the different practices of the team members. It becomes clear what the differences are in handling the questions on different levels and whether this works for others or not. This leads to the intention to stop certain ways of working and then transforms into decisions in the day-to-day work.

By continuing in the research mode—rather than jumping to conclusions and actions by starting to propose programs immediately—the ongoing dialogue is revived and invigorated and can be continued even outside the working environment. Many unusual activities are now taking place: explorations, discussions, interactions, engagement and learning. People are, together with others, trying out new courses of actions and procedures in their practical business life.

I will illustrate this with the help of a short case description of one of the participating organisations:

"A Healthcare organization with a number of doctors' offices and nursing homes, grouped by regional divisions, participated in this process with a team formed by the regional director, one head of a nursing home, two team leaders and two co-workers. The question that quickly emerged was the issue of client-centered working. One of the co-workers remarked that the issue had already been on the table for more than 15 years, but that she had seen very little actual change. The team starts discussing various real cases. One of these is about an elderly lady who is not allowed to smoke in the house anymore due to the new fire regulations. One of the nurses takes the lady out once in a while, so they can smoke a cigarette together. This irritates the colleagues. After they have been debating this incident for a while, the question of client-centered working transforms into the issue of how their work can be performed with more personal attention towards the client and for each other. When the issue was openly discussed in the nursing homes, both clients and staff reacted with vehemence. "The issue of attention" became more important in the day-to-day practice. Immediately, the team was reflecting on how to further improve this aspect and examined new ways of dealing with the client. Reality, however, showed that paying more personal attention to

the needs of their clients was a difficult, if not impossible, issue to structure in an organized approach. Nevertheless, by intensifying the process of research and experiment and by stepping up the engagement sessions with still more people in the organization, the issue started to show signs of betterment in the work process. The improvements were also experienced in the wider community of staff members, by the clients, their families and the professionals."

Tell me what we must do

A female executive runs this very big national institute dealing with almost all citizens in the country. Spread over the whole country there are branch offices with thousands of employees. The institute has a good reputation and is constantly trying to improve its service and operational processes. When she started the job, she made a critical evaluation of the institute's state. Are the change processes effective in the institute? Do the many projects running deliver sufficient returns? Are enough co-workers involved in the change processes or are too many of them being left out? Can we continue with this operational structure or do we need to change it?

She decides to step up the change process for the whole of the institute. The top management agrees to commit themselves as process owners of this change. The idea is to improve customer service, implement self-steering teams and restructure the institute into regional units.

She drives the process with a vision. The core of her vision is the motto: *"We will do it together."* The services for the different segments of customers are integrated in a regional office, which is run by a change management team. Team leaders and their teams have to reflect about their work processes from the customer service perspective. They are challenged to improve these processes. Staff departments have to review their own services critically.

"Do not wait for the others, forge ahead," she encourages the regions and teams. Managers with good ideas can test them in their own region. The whole process is based on managers and co-workers taking initiatives, deciding their next step for themselves, communicating with each other, taking responsibility. The board appreciates that there is a space for freedom and accepts that not every place will display the same working style. The whole organization is very aware of the vision of the director-general. However, many of the employees do not know how to deal with that vision.

"Tell us what we must do," is a common question. The reply they receive is as follows: *"First you have to think yourself and only then talk to me to ask questions."*

Says the director-general: *"I want to get rid of those who only pretend to know better and decide what is right. We need to do it together because we depend on each other to fulfill our task. First of all, we should ensure that our processes are running smoothly and can be handled by both our employees and the customers together. The employees can bring in their own ideas and the leadership should listen to these ideas and help them to be implemented when they make sense. They can adapt their own organization to their specific situation without us losing the overall control. We do not need all kinds of highly skilled specialists to tell us what is best. Let us identify the conditions, which give people the chance to decide what might be best for us. I realize that maybe not everybody might grasp this opportunity. But if we do not challenge each other now, we will not take the right steps. I am not fully aware how this approach will work out in the end, but I do see other expert approaches failing in all kinds of organizations. I believe in using the intelligence of our own people. Our self-confidence will grow. We will continue our history of development and change. For as long as I have worked here, I have seen impulses for change. I hope that will stay this way."*

Case story 3: The pharmaceutical company

The third example is about a fast-growing pharmaceutical company in Germany.

In this organization, they develop and produce medicine and cosmetics based on natural ingredients. The quality of the products is so convincing for the customers using them that even famous movie stars promote these products for free. This organization has displayed a strong growth pattern over the years. As a consequence, a lot of energy was needed to support this growth. Top management is worried that one day the organization will get stuck and will not be able to handle the process properly. They debated the issue and asked themselves the question: "What do we see as the next step we want this organization to take?"

They arranged for a special process in which the different parts of the company would examine how the flow of the operational processes and the cooperation among each other could be improved and how the decision making could be performed more elegantly.

Looking at the interfaces

The first points to look at were the interfaces between departments like development, sales and marketing, production and infrastructure, and how these interfaces were working in day-to-day operations. In small teams, managers and co-workers started this analysis together. Soon they discovered that the company tended to work very much in a top-down and bottom-up way and that, as a result, the higher hierarchical echelons were under high pressure. As there was relatively little interaction at the same levels, they started to experiment with a horizontal way of working. It quickly became clear that the leadership of the middle management, department heads and team leaders had to be strongly involved in this process of horizontal cooperation.

Strengthening the leadership

As a second step, the process of strengthening the leadership itself was introduced. This process started with the 360° analysis of the middle management's competencies in horizontal leadership and how they operated in the horizontal space. All managers participated in a coaching process, in which they shared their leadership issues with each other. How do I energize my staff, how do I make my personal position clear, how can I be confrontational? How can I identify bottlenecks in the work processes in time and support people to change them? By working on these questions, they discovered the need for a clear focus. The customer and the customer process were seen as the key focus to concentrate on while, at the same time, improving the organizational processes and cooperation.

The customer process

Finally, a third process was launched: this process was directed at changing the interactions with the customers. Are we going to serve all potential customer segments or do we want our products to be only available to the customers with an understanding and an appreciation of them? The organization responded to the market demand with a policy of selective supply. Specialized shops were the preferred sales channel because representatives in the shop could advise the consumer on the best application of the product. The products worked much better and, as a result, left the customer much happier and more satisfied when he received proper instructions and advice before the purchase. It is about a process of self healing most of the time. Mass markets were to be avoided. The company's absolute priority of remaining in the highest quality market segment had to be respected.

Working in a rhythmic way

Senior management enters a regular engagement with others. Due to the continuous process of researching with other managers and staff, a desire to rather work according to a specific rhythm in all processes emerges. For instance, the process for production planning is transformed from hectic to rhythmic. The agitated and confused style in many different meetings is transformed into a rhythmic way of holding them. Finding the appropriate rhythm is the art of leadership.

The process of developing and launching new products in the market, a process which involves almost all departments of the company, is placed in the hands of process owners responsible for a more elegant and smooth process of decision making. This decision making process has agreed milestones along the timeline for taking the next step, and the different phases of the process are identified and marked. The process requires a consistent concentration and continuous simplification.

The remarkable outcome of these processes has been that there is a much more relaxed atmosphere in the company, a greater transparency and an intensive horizontal dialogue. The structural bottlenecks are exposed and the organization is better equipped to anticipate which production, marketing and logistic capacities are needed to overcome them. The community building process as a leadership process turns out to be a crucial one in handling the further development and growth of the company.

Conclusion

These three stories show how horizontal leadership in practice enables and empowers all the people who should participate and work in the process of change in a beneficial way.

It is also by this kind of interesting example shown how it is not an automatism that managers also act as true leaders. This now poses the question: Why is this the case? It is important to understand this, as we still tend to see managers as leaders of people, and so we give them the people to lead—without being sure of their actual competencies in this field. We carried out some research concerning this issue and I will share the key findings from this research with you.

Do we really understand what leadership is about, how it works and why that is the case?

A leadership experience:
The bank director

After merging a city bank with a regional bank, the managing director of the regional bank, who had worked there for many years, was asked to become the new overall managing director of the new entity. He was confident that he could leave his mark on the newly merged company, and was looking forward to the whole new challenge of leading a bank with over 3,000 employees.

After the completion of the technical and legal merger, however, it became obvious that the result was not yet one company with a single culture. Both parts continued working in their own, very different ways, just as they had before the merger. The city bank had strict and directive procedures and systems with most of the power of decision highly centralized, whilst the regional bank relied much more on the entrepreneurship of its staff.

To start a process of creating one common style and culture, the general director defines four projects for development.

The central project is about customer service: "The bank is for our clients."

The second project is about team spirit: "We are in it all together."

The third project is about performance: "We want to rank with the best."

The fourth project is about the future: "Our young colleagues will be fully involved in the process."

The general director chooses, together with his colleagues from the board, the process owners, who will take up these four change processes for the whole bank. It is their responsibility to work through these themes (projects) and involve whoever is necessary to achieve the planned results.

An example: There are 120 branch offices with a common set-up, having the same structure and similarly trained staff. They all follow the same procedures and work with the same IT systems and, in particular, offer the same range of products and services. However, customers from an affluent area expect a different kind of offer as those with a less wealthy background. Their varying lifestyles require different responses to their individual needs. The development process encourages the different sales offices to adapt their offer to their clients' needs and requirements. Specialized bank employees are being trained to help with specific customer demands. The standard product range is simplified and the systems are adapted accordingly.

The process owners engage many of their colleagues in the bank to participate in and contribute towards the various projects. The projects are run in parallel to the normal operational work in the bank. Hundreds of young colleagues are invited to take up a project in their own team to improve their performance. The criteria for the projects are that they should add value to the customer process, the results of the team and individual learning. The young employees can design, execute and evaluate the project on their own, they can invite other colleagues to contribute and involve experts from the central office to give them some specialized support. The process owners coach and monitor these projects. They support the project members taking the initiative and handle any bottlenecks. The whole process creates a certain degree of turmoil and anxiety in the bank.

The bank director:

"When I took up my job, it was my intention to turn the two banks, each with their own style and ways of working, into one single entity—as quickly as possible. I am mainly concerned about customers and performance; I do not much like problems. My idea was that we have a very competent body of staff eager to deliver. But I also encountered rather strict ways of working, which was very limiting to personal initiative. I got rather upset when I realized what was going on around us and I saw many of us rather sleepwalking through our work than actively progressing towards our targets. I wanted to see much more dynamics in this bank. Not just passively waiting for customers, but rather make an active connection with them. Not only to concentrate on one's own job, but also assist colleagues when the work process requires it. I enjoy meeting employees who tell me about their initiatives, putting their ideas into practice. I learn from them. When the young co-workers present their projects and results to the board, it makes my heart happy. That inspires me the most. Sure: the department heads still place many problems on my table. I tend to take the issues up myself to see what results from my actions. But I also understand that it is more sensible to help them to deal with their issues themselves. I can coach them, but they need to actually resolve it themselves. Then, the new generation of leaders will learn from example to act on their own account and will become eager to do so. They have been involved in different processes and know how to handle complex processes. For instance, to see the young controller who not only supplies the figures but also shows his colleagues how to apply them in their work and make sense of them.

CHAPTER 7: # Key findings in our horizontal leadership research

Now, I would like to share some of the key findings in our horizontal leadership research with you.

The most essential findings are:

1. Leadership requires for its community building and Sense-Making a certain "image of man" as basis.
2. Leadership is based on a personally developed leadership vision.
3. Leadership uses a different language than the hierarchical management language we are used to in organizations.
4. Leadership is about creating change and innovation through the process of Sense-Making in organizations.

1. Leadership requires for its community building and Sense-Making a certain "image of man" as basis

Leadership can be seen as part of the process of community building and how we make sense of the things we create. This is primarily done on the basis of the image of man that is living in each one of us. These images can be very limited or can be of a much broader perspective. We can see man as an operative machine that follows the orders and produces the desired results. We can also see man as a creative individual that makes free decisions as to where and how to commit himself to the role that is taken. In leadership, we deal with different people with different views on man and we try to achieve our ideals together. The way leadership is performed strongly influences how members of the community treat each other and how they interact to meet their targets. The quality of the leadership determines the quality of the relationships between those within the community. That can be mainly relationships of power, but also of developments, research or creativity. In leadership we express the image that we have of our fellow man.

2. Leadership is based on a personally developed leadership vision

Based on our horizontal leadership research, we have gained some insights into how leadership is developed in the community by leaders. These are:

There is no single "best way" of leadership; it works simply on the basis of a very personal repertoire. Whereas for the hierarchical version of management many concepts, models and tool kits have been developed and are being practiced on a broad scale today, there is no such thing for leadership.

Leadership is directed towards leading people and how they cooperate in the community. The leadership process works in an interactive and horizontal way. In that sense, it is not functionally embedded in the hierarchy, but it only works between persons in an open, non-structured space.

Leadership is determined by the authentic personality of the leader. The biographical connection between person and organization is of great meaning and impact in how the leadership will work. Does an individual's personality, which is active in a leadership process, become visible in the context of the values and culture of this organization?

Leadership is a process in which we can participate and in which we try to realize our intents, ideas and motives. It is a process on the basis of individuals inviting others to participate. We involve each other in the leadership process.

Every person develops a personal leadership story. Our leadership story develops within us through an individual leadership learning process. By reflecting on our experiences, sharing these reflections with others and giving them our own sense, we develop and strengthen our own leadership abilities and competencies.

Leaders have developed their own image of man that shows itself in the way they deal with other people and involve them in the leadership process. This image of man which the leader has developed affects the way the leader performs. When we have an open image of man, which means that we are not fixated on the way we see the other person and deal with this person, there is for us an open space in the leadership process for how we deal with each other.

Management, primarily, has a specific system orientation on how they deal with the human reality to achieve a correct and consistent operation of work processes. Leadership, however, is pivoted on another axis, as it handles the differences and utilizes them in the leadership process. The aim and art of leadership is to turn the differences within an organization into benefits for the development and change processes.

Leadership is directed towards the development of man and organization. It shifts people and processes to new and different places by concentrating on the development of work processes, human abilities and insights, by means of stimulating research and experimentation. As a consequence, the individuals as well as the organization as a whole can integrate new ways of working into the organizational reality.

Leadership is a process of Sense-Making that adds rationality to the creations we make as human beings. In the operational processes we are forced to act out of the discipline needed in the working environment. In change and development processes, however, we are challenged to think about the "what", "how" and "why". We can add sense through these development processes so that the operations can be carried out tomorrow in a different way and with a different perspective.

3. Leadership language

Leadership moves to the head of the processes of research and experimentation and draws the conclusions for what this means for the operational work processes and structures. Leading personalities communicate in an easily understood verbal and sign/body language with the many other people involved in the process. It is not the same language that we find in the management jargon which has already been developed to a great degree. It does not use the construed systems language management uses nowadays. Leadership is using an elementary human language. We find in this language words such as attention or caring, trust, connecting, playing together, loving and passion, motivation, learning, responsibility. These human qualities can not be ordained by management. Leadership language cannot be shaped in a functional way; we cannot create any standard conditions to make that happen. It is not working on the basis of power. The language already gives us the answer that these words have their own connotations. We can only speak of *paying* attention, *earning* trust, *developing* or *instilling* motivation, *making* a connection, *being* passionate, *taking* responsibility. This can only be born out of the inner world of the individual, out of his own personality. And it will only work between authentic people. Therefore, it is not in the hands of management but in the hands of leadership. Leadership in itself is *given* and *taken*, it is a dialogical process, and *we lead each other.*

4.   Leadership is about creating change

Change processes are about creating a new balance between our thoughts and actions, which works hand in hand. The process of change is taking place in us while we support each other and share trust, pay attention to and care for each other, make the connections, learn from each other, and create sense. In the change processes we address the unresolved issues, the inner life of ourselves and the other. We can take a step forward with our unresolved issues, which is hard for us to do in the vertical operational reality. There is no place for such a step in a vertical hierarchy.

When the top leaders are not only outwardly committed to the change issues but feel these issues as a inner obligation as well, and when middle management is empowered to explore the horizontal space and to participate in the horizontal leadership, changes *can* happen and be brought about in the context of the horizontal leadership process. This will help the organization to move into the future and find the continuation of its existence. One important proviso, however, is that the issues and new steps make sense for those working at the customer interface and for the customers themselves. This is the conclusion we have drawn from of our research on horizontal leadership, which we have done over many years in more than twenty organizations of various kinds in different countries.

Sense-Making and leadership

One of the most important dimensions of leadership we discovered is the Sense-Making to individuals of an organization. The man-made structure we call organization does not have sense in itself because it is unable to exist and continue existing without consistent human actions. When we maintain our creations it requires a continuous investment of energy and resources. What is created only is given its sense when we use it for the continuation of our existence. If we do not continue to add sense to it, then it immediately loses its sense. Every product, structure, procedure or policy looses sense if we do not infuse sense into it—again and again.

We can ask ourselves the question of how sense is actually generated.

Our observation is that sense is not created by more action and programs and projects, but comes into existence through reflection and dialogue. Sense-Making is coming about within us by the inner investigations we undertake. To achieve this, we have to reserve inner and outer spaces for reflection and Sense-Making in organizations.

In our society we have managed to virtually destroy all the Sense-Making spaces we used to have. There is no Sunday anymore, we have skipped the breaks, there is no dialogue for just the joy of dialogue. Everything is lined up for a specific chosen target. It is not the done thing anymore to make a non-productive move. Everything has to fit, lead somewhere and—most importantly—be successful. Real life, however, also includes failure, frustration, a set-back. In organizations this is not permitted, we cannot accept failure and we have to avoid this happening under all circumstances. That is expected of us.

Real leadership is there to restore the spaces for Sense-Making and give them a meaning in the organizational context. Leadership asks the question concerning the roots of the organization and how to safeguard them. What is this organization for, what is the core of its existence, how do we integrate the new and preserve the tradition at the same time?

We are often faced with the fact that our lives have become a paradox. By allowing for a break to research, reflect and learn, we discover the sense of what keeps us so busy all the time. "Sense" is not intrinsically a part of the action itself, the program or the project, but sense is coming out of what we reflectively add to our actions (Karl Weick). It gives us valuable stories telling us what is going on inside of us. In this respect, my definition of leadership is: "Not doing more, but creating a process in which others can add sense to what they are doing."

It is through Sense-Making that we shape our future; we prepare ourselves to face the new and the different. This requires seeing the new generations arriving, seeing different desires and longings, seeing the new competencies we need to develop to live in a sensible world.

Summing up

Management is something entirely different than leadership. Management is the organizing of the operations with the help of systems. It works functionally and vertically.

Leadership is the creation of the next development step, which works through the Sense-Making horizontal dialogue.

In leadership we work with our individually developed leadership concepts and visions. Horizontal leadership works best in organizations, when all the different hierarchical levels are involved in the leadership process together.

It is the customer process and the leadership process which are the key decisive processes in an organization because the ultimate value is created in an interactive process, in which things are not fully predefined or predetermined. There exists an open space, which permits us to act and reflect. These two processes form the core of the process of community building in organizations and it is here that the inner world of our personal individuality plays a central role. Our personal barriers and desires, too, are being affected. This is reflected in the leadership language as we mentioned before. These qualities are not relevant in the process of organizing operations, but they play an essential role in the process of man and organizational development.

It is recommended to attempt to begin with the horizontal dialogue in a specifically designed process that opens up the community and makes it accessible to new processes. Otherwise, one might find that many problems do not translate immediately or quickly into infrastructural solutions and yet more systems could be implemented, stifling internal operations and making any progress most cumbersome. Instead of management taking continuous measures to control various issues, it would be wiser to ask more questions that lead to a common reflection on phenomena observed.

Instead of more actions, programs and projects to tackle the problems, it would be wiser to first research and experiment with the fundamental questions and invite members from many different levels of the community to participate in the process.

We should thus challenge the many top-down managed change programs that often have little effect and tend to fail.

It does not work to *tell* others to look in the same direction, but it makes more sense to create a process, developed and led by committed process owners, in which everybody involved can make a personal step in dealing with the issue.

It is advisable to seek the inclusion of the customer to find out how the organizational processes affect them and, in a dialogue with him, arrive at good ideas leading to improvement and innovation.

A leadership experience:
The unit manager

A sales organization is being changed. Sales operations are divided into two units. Each unit works on specific markets, located in different parts of the world and selling different products. Each unit has a front and back office. There is also a logistics unit taking care of delivery and transport.

One of the sales staff is nominated as sales unit manager of a sales unit. During the first year, he had to get used to his new role amongst his former colleagues. He tended to be the critical person and now suddenly finds himself being responsible. He is not too enthusiastic about the sales director as a leader and manager. They are both pretty young, ambitious and have a fairly competitive attitude.

The sales director forms the sales management team together with the other unit managers. He is very good at analyzing the market portfolios and he redistributes them among his units. This is a useful initiative. The cooperation between front and back office is also crucial. When the sales reps are out in the field, the back office keeps the customer contact going. He creates miniteams of three, by assigning to each sales rep from the front office one customer service agent from the back office and one logistics specialist. They are held responsible for the whole end-to-end process of sales and delivery for each individual customer.

Within the unit itself, operations run smoothly, however, problems arise with units in other departments. The research and development department teams are too much left to their own devices and also production is not sufficiently on the radar screen. Staff from central organization is initiating many complex projects, such as centralizing supply, creating a new brand name or defining a new product strategy, installing central planning and budgeting.

The sales unit manager finds himself faced with a heavy overload. He decides to focus on the unit sales targets, the planning process and the execution of the sales activities. In his opinion, planning and budgeting must be realistic. But the company's general manager is pushed by higher forces to raise the sales quota by an extra 10%. The sales unit manager believes that the company has already reached its limit on its sales performance and is therefore reluctant to take on this additional target. The managing director tries to find a compromise between central interests and the company's interests. The tension rises to such a level that the sales unit manager explodes. He wants to protect his team and he does not want to be bullied by the central office staff.

The situation leads to a few confrontational meetings with the managing director, in which the sales staff's emotions run high. In the end, they do find a solution. The managing director reviews this event together with the sales unit manager and points out to him that he needs to control himself more in the face of the external parties.

The sales unit manager:

"Well, I think I have to stand up for my team. We went through our planning and budget process in the best possible way. We have a highly motivated team and have returned the best results in sales. We are the ones standing in the line of fire: we are talking with the customers, we know the market and we can judge what the market potential is. The demands of the central organization are unbalanced and not reasonable. We simply cannot accept this procedure. I understand that our general manager has to be diplomatic. I know he is also upset by the demands from the central organization. It was very bad that we got into this kind of confrontational position. I am happy that we afterwards were able to resolve the affair together in a constructive manner. I have learned that I was communicating with the upper levels in an inappropriate fashion. I do not like compromises. But I understand that my loyalty cannot only lie with my own team. I have to take other claims seriously, especially within the line of hierarchy. I am happy, however, that I stood my ground on this. But I still have to keep all communication channels open with the others as well. What counts in the end is a good result, which can accommodate everybody.

CHAPTER 8: # Images of the development of man as a basis for leadership learning

I would like to focus on the internal aspect of the leadership issue. The internal aspect is to be understood as the inner values, orientations and intentions felt by the leading persons. These values, orientations and intentions are very much influenced by the perception and attitude the person has of the "image of man"—constituting a paradigm, which a person will form in the course of his life and which will over time become ever deeper ingrained in his personality. This happens through a process of transition, experienced in the own biography.

The leadership requires for this transition a consistent process of personal development by which the individual can become a more authentic person with a solid foundation to meet the leadership challenges.

I first want to share some examples on the "images of man" with you, which will help you understand this conception of the human being and its path of development. You can study these images of man and man-in-transition and internalize them as part of your personal development path. If you wish to carry the responsibility as a leader, it challenges you to develop towards a good and wise person who is in touch with your own biography, as well as the biographies of the others you cooperate with.

1. Looking at your fellow man

The main source for personal leadership development learning is facing "man itself".

One can look at the human being in many different ways. This depends greatly on the individual perspective and also on what are the dominant paradigms in reflecting on these observations. I would like to describe here some of the most dominant images or ways of looking at man, with which we are familiar in dealing with each other in the organizational context.

In the reality of day-to-day life, the image of man we carry in us is most explicit in the way we treat others and also ourselves. We sometimes have little appreciation and understanding of the way we regard others. This can for instance be seen when managers deal with their co-workers and with each other in an inconsistent and impulsive way. I have observed on many occasions that managers tend to complain about the level of motivation of their staff. They speak about them as people who wouldn't budge without instructions from management. These people frequently react by showing reluctance to be pushed around. When, however, the same manager regards him/herself, there is hardly ever the self-perception of lacking motivation. In my research, with the help of leadership research questionnaires, I have noticed a *structural* difference in how managers judge themselves versus their judgment they pass on others they work with. However, I have also observed that when there is space in the heart of a manager to see this disparity in his way of looking at others and at him or herself, then there grows a better understanding of how the personal leadership can work in a fruitful way for other people at work.

1.1. The historic man

A first way of looking at man that is described here is the image that man is a continuation of his ancestors. Man is a result of his forbearers. As the saying goes: The apple does not fall far from the tree. You look like your parents; your siblings have much in common with you. Who you are, your character, your inner world, your individual and personal traits will probably, to a very large extent, resemble those of your parents and grandparents. Standing in this tradition gives you a strong connection to the family you belong to. You have the same genes, you share the same language and cultural/religious background. Your whole being is strongly influenced by your roots.

In this way, man's individuality is predetermined. At the time of your birth, your DNA is already irreversibly cast in stone and will greatly decide what kind of person you will be. This will appropriate you physically and mentally to your ancestors. This image is typical for communities of casts, kingships, professions, et cetera, whereby you could only live together with people of your own level and class and social background. People like Darwin and Freud used this image of man as a basis for further exploration of the human psyche. In neurochemical science one can be enthusiastic about manipulating human genes. The aim is to improve the nature of the human race. On a symposium in London in 1962, there were discussions around the theme of "manipulating the human factor to support the opportunity to create more useful versions of the human species."

This stance was maybe typical for the pre-industrial phase. You had to respond to your personal heritage. The biological but also religious/ethical background dominated the perspectives you had in life. It was difficult to break through the barriers this image imposed. After today's ascension of science and also the industrial age there was a strong challenge to overthrow this image of man.

This view on man is challenged by the empirics. They see man as being born like a weak animal that is not so much destined by genetic inheritance but has to be shaped and formed during life. Without cultural education there is no need for the baby to rise and stand and speak, only the instinct to survive would be at work.

This is the second image of man.

1.2. Man as "tabula rasa"

Man is born as an untouched white page of a book, in which life will inscribe itself, said John Locke. During man's life, the surroundings and experiences engrave themselves into the personality of a human being. It makes a great difference whether you are raised in a royal family or in a poor man's working environment. In spite of this, man is flexible and capable to adapt: he can move in different directions and is not bound to his roots. He can take up any profession, as long as he acquires the necessary competencies by training and education. Skinner is one of the most prominent protagonists of this view. He researched the process of man's formation. It is about stimulus and response processes. These processes are the most effective when there is a reward promised which is connected to a response to the stimulus. This image of man has been very influential in how we can make organizations work for people: for instance by creating the appropriate labor conditions so that man is motivated to do what is required. Skinner and also Pavlov believed that man as an intelligent animal can overcome his instinct and perform different types of behavior to be able to attain the reward. The difference to the animal in my view, however, is that man can also act in this way without expecting any promised reward.

This image of man is the intellectual foundation for a lot of training programs and the shaping of people's behavior.

This image of man adopts the idea that people can be changed. There is a scientific evidence for this image of the human being created by psychological scientists. Many psychological theories and therapies are based on this idea that you must first break down "the old personality" and then rebuild "the new personality". There are complete social cultures based on this specific picture of man. The personality is formed to respond to the ideology that is underlying political convictions or that man is thrown into, and formed by an organization with certain company values and behavior patterns. Man can be influenced and even manipulated to the extent that his actions become pro-grammed and predictable. All heads can be turned in the same direction. To conform to the rules and to make man fit into the picture is part of this image of man. "Fit in or fuck off" is maybe the strongest expression of this image of man.

In reaction to this image of man there was the rise of "personalism", which stresses the individual unique personality as the core of the human be-ing. The personalists would point out that there is still something else in the game: human personality.

1.3. The unique human being

Man can also be seen as a unique individuality, a unique personality, the only one in the cosmos completely like him—there is no identical specimen of the very kind! No person can be compared to another. There will always be a dif-ference. Every individual has a specific expression and the development of the personality can never be fully predicted. Man can push through boundaries, overcome the laws of destiny and create a free space of personal development; that is what this image of man says. Man can set his own goals and make his own steps. It is the force and strength of the individual human spirit that makes this possible. There is a higher "I" at work in the person that can make choices and develop specific values and norms for the individual life. It is only the individual person that has the specific ability to experience him/herself and reflect on this experience and learn from it. After being born into this life, the individual personality starts a process of becoming more visible and more active and he or she can be in an ever-ongoing process of growth, development and transformation. This is an existentialist standpoint.

1.4. Man as a multiple being

In my view, it is of the greatest value for leadership today to be able to see man as a multiple being representing all these different images as they stand for the different aspects of man. Whilst it is quite evident that you have only one father and one mother, as far as birth is concerned, it can also be said that from a spiritual point of view, you can have other personalities and mentors giving you direction in life. As an individual you will have the freedom to choose the person you want to take your lead in life. This view of seeing the human being as a multiple being opens up to a broader view on the fundamentals of the human constitution.

The issue of the image of man has been a growing point of ethical awareness and has led to debate, since we all have come to live more in the organized community and become more conscious how this effects us as a person.

Some see the human being purely as a physical body and thus, everything in that respect is a bodily function. Everything is produced, so to say, by the body. "We need the hands to do the job," is the credo. Others see man purely as spiritual. It is only the sprit that is reality and all else is unreal. So it is the vision which drives and inspires us—it is the vision that makes things happen. Then there is also the vision that man is soul and that it is only our individual thought, emotions and will which make the human being part of the wider community.

In my opinion, however, it could very well be that we embody all three of these aspects. We are body, soul and spirit. We are a beautiful composition of these three "components". This broadens the leadership perspective, meeting other people and taking a path of development and change together.

How would this work?

With our *"physical body"* we can work and experience the senses and the effect they have on others. With our senses we are able to observe and experience the world around us. But we can also experience the quality of thinking and how memory works in us. We can reflect on our experiences, add a certain meaning to them. We can feel the effect others have on us, and we can become active because we decide to do so.

The *"soul"* is coming into existence. To really understand and see what we see, we have to be in a process of exploring and do this each time in a little different way.

And it is here that we find the *"spirit"* becoming involved. It is the world of ideas and forces behind the observables that we start to explore with our spirit. It is opening up the entrance for us into unknown territory; it helps us to look into the future and really understand the past.

When we can start to see man as this multiple being that is able to connect to totally different realities, we create a valuable ability to make these connections in the practice of our life. We can start to better understand how things work inside and between people and also between people and the worlds that are around and within us.

2.   Crisis and transition in the biography

The path to understanding ourselves and others is not always a path lined with roses. It is a path on which we are confronted again and again with a life that is different from what we think it is.

The path towards horizontal self-leadership is not without barriers, which must be overcome—not only in the observable outside world, but first and foremost in the inner world of ourselves. We have to deal with crisis and transition in our biography.

Transitions start with an end.

It is you saying goodbye to the old well-known.

That is happening because there is an impulse for change from within you or from outside you.

You react very differently to these impulses for change. You become angry, paralyzed or silent.

After the first shock, the mood can improve and you neglect the need for change and minimize the impact it has on your life.

But fear and anxiety are close under the surface.

The outside world gets the blame of the pain that you feel inside.

To get angry does not help in the end, you are alone with it, you have reached the bottom of the well.

Then there is the crisis.

That is a period of self-confrontation and reflection.

You start to see: the past is not coming back.

There is no clear vision of the future.

The old solutions do not work anymore.

Putting the blame on others does not help anymore.

Analyzing it constantly makes it worse.

That someone is going to give you a solution is no longer expected.

The idea enters the mind that you have to do it all by yourself.

A step into the unknown.

The individual "I" is still weak and that is sensed strongly.

There is a new beginning.
> *Small steps are taken.*
> *You experiment with the unknown.*
> *There is learning from new experiences.*
> *What did I want to do, what did I do, what is the effect, what is the next step?*
> *You meet different people than before.*
> *You connect yourself mentally with the new situation.*
> *There is drive and motivation and growing interest.*
> *There is an integration of all the new in your own personality.*
> *The old appears in the new.*

It is only partly possible for oneself to steer this process of transition.

We can see three steps that can help the person to go through this process.

1. The first is that you take the situation seriously—not only with your head but also your heart and body. It is important to fully experience in oneself the thoughts, emotions and frustrations, and not to suppress them.

2. To do this, it is important to differentiate between facts and feelings. Emotions will influence you and accordingly taint what is observed. It does not make sense to jump to solutions, but it is more important to find the right people, who can help you to identify with the change and to whom you can express your emotions. Exerting yourself physically doing sports or exercises to handle the energy level can help you to balance the bad and energy-sapping feelings.

3. This must be connected to a sense of moral duty to take on the challenge and make yourself responsible for what is happening.

In the leadership process, organizations and their management can open up to a better understanding and feeling for the transition process, which people involved experience when they and the organization go through a process of change. For leadership to see and accept that this transition process takes place in the people in the organization and in themselves would be of great help in steering the change process. It can help all people tremendously to grow and become ever stronger through this experience when it is taken seriously in the leadership process creating change. Just as we in our private life must accept that there is crisis and transition, we can learn to do the same in our organizations; as living communities where people meet their destiny.

This learning is part of a process to develop as a person towards horizontal leadership. The competence of horizontal leadership is the solid basis on which people can act as leaders in the community. How can that work?

3. The educational path towards horizontal leadership

The biography we live, the road of life that we walk on is unique and is embroidered with our personal confrontations and challenges. During life, we are confronted with failure, with battle and conflict, with set-backs. But also we are met by temptations and we are plunging into unknown adventures. All this appeals to our personality, our "I". We are tested to see whether we can stand up to the challenges and temptations. We are given the opportunity to develop as a person. We are able to teach ourselves, learn from experience. Man can invest in himself and become his own instrument. We can take an educational path towards horizontal leadership.

3.1. The practical path of learning

The practical educational path towards horizontal leadership is: learning from life. Every life situation we encounter holds a learning opportunity as well. We are tested all the time whether we can face life and keep our head above water. We can learn from others how to do this. But in the leadership moment we are on our own and have to deal both with the situation and ourselves. This is a process in which time, space, connections and money are involved, in which we can take initiatives, reflect on our values and connect to our spiritual existence. This practical path of education is reflected in the biography we live. It is a process of self-steering. That is not the easiest thing to do.

In the organized world we live in, we are confronted with many others, who often want to decide on the path of our life. We, for instance, feel a lack of time and resources to meet all the challenges and invitations of people, who want or at least expect something of us. In the leadership we must learn to deal with these real dimensions of life in the personal and organized life. We are challenged to master our time, our money, our network, our space.

3.2. Mastering our time

The first challenge is to master your time. To master time, you have to start to understand the processes you are living in and handle them in a process-oriented fashion. In which direction should I move, which pattern of life do I keep on living—maybe despite a lot in it not really being relevant anymore? Can I move myself to be ahead of the game or will I always be too late? If one looks at the pattern of a week, it is very interesting to ask oneself the question, does this travel in time have a rhythm in which you meet realities you want to be in, or do you find yourself in realities you do not want to be part of?

3.3. Mastering our money

Not only time but also money determines our life. What is the money we earn and how do we spend this money? Do I spend this money on things and activities I find important, or is money running through my fingers and I can not see where it has gone? Money reflects a lot of our decisions and it mirrors what we do in practice. Very often money is spent on things we should instead have said goodbye to a long time ago. To balance money and handle it with a conscious mind helps to enter life situations which are good for us to be in.

3.4. Mastering our network

A third dimension of life education towards horizontal self leadership is the handling of the networks of people you are relating to and sharing life with. Who are the people in your network and what do they stand for? Is it family or colleagues, or is it specific individuals you share a certain interest with? Are you spending your life with people you feel close to, or are you surrounded by people you are not really connected to? Can you develop such a relation to the other person that it makes sense to both of you and fulfills a deep common interest?

3.5. Mastering our space

A fourth dimension is physical space. What are the spaces you live and move in, the offices, houses, cars, et cetera? How do you move in these spaces? Are you actually occupying these spaces or are you moving close to the walls? It is a wonderful life quality to decorate the spaces that are yours. Do you decorate your office space, for instance, or is it an anonymous space, in which anybody could be?

It is very relevant to ask yourself these questions and start to see how to shape them in your private and your work life. For many of us, these dimensions are determined by others and we feel powerless to change them. It is through the learning process in our practical life that we can master them in time and create the solid basis for our own leadership. This learning can be intensified when we are open to the many insights of others whom we trust and whom we can learn from. Our personal leadership learning is also intensified when we reflect on our experiences, when we dialogue with others about them and gain some insights, which can become the lights that shine on our path.

3.6. The spiritual path of learning

There is another path of educating our personal leadership that we can call the spiritual path of learning.

Bernard Lievegoed describes this in his book "Ways of initiation".

He speaks of a Moon path and a Saturn path.

The Moon path

The moon path is an individual path of meditation. We can educate our soul by educating our ability to think, to feel and to will. We can educate our thinking by going through concentration exercises. We can educate our feeling by meeting the other with a positive attitude and by developing empathy. We can educate our free will by acting out a deed that is only born inside of us because we find it important to do. By exercising these soul forces, we strengthen ourselves for the process of handling the challenges of life through personal leadership. There have been many mystery schools of initiation that have supported people following the moon path.

The saturn path

The moon path is a very old path that is widely known to have been followed throughout the long history of man. The saturn path is relatively new and is linked to our organized life of today. We live and work in organizations and we are challenged to connect our personal biography to the biography of these organizations. Organizations are creating new communities of people meeting their destiny in these communities. By taking responsibility for the development of these organized communities, we meet our soul companions with whom we can share our deepest ideals and strivings. We connect ourselves to other people sharing a common spiritual orientation in how we want to handle life. When I deepen the impulses, I experience and connect them to the impulses of organizations that in turn want to serve the customer / other human beings, then I am connecting myself to a collective path of learning and growing: the horizontal self-leadership path.

Today, the practical way of education and the spiritual way of educating ourselves in personal leadership come together for each person having the intention to follow the educational path. This path is wonderfully expressed by the story of Percival.

The legend of Percival

Percival is born into a noble family. His father, a knight, died after many battles when he was finally mortally wounded. His mother then moves into the woods and tries to protect Percival and to prevent him from becoming a knight himself. One day, however, Percival meets four knights in the woods and these knights shine so brightly that Percival thinks he has met God. This impression is so overwhelming that Percival decides to leave his mother and to start the search for this gleaming light. His mother is so sad that she dies soon after Percival has left. A long path lies ahead of Percival. His mother had taught Percival his manners, to pray and to be polite. That is what Percival does. However, he experiences situations he does not understand and in which he acts foolishly because of it. When he kisses a sleeping woman he finds very beautiful, he naturally angers the husband of this woman. Percival flees and rushes to King Arthur's castle to become a knight. There he meets a red knight, who challenges him. He kills the knight and takes his horse and clothes. He meets another knight in his wonderful castle, who teaches him how to fight. "Do not speak too much," is the lesson he learns from this knight.

At a certain moment in the legend, he comes upon a mysterious castle. When he arrives there, the bridge comes down and he passes the bridge. He is welcomed and led to a beautiful room. There are new clothes and he can refresh himself. He then is invited to enter the main hall. There are many people standing there and strange things happen right before Percival's eyes. In the middle of the hall sits King Amfortas who is clearly wounded. A spear is carried through the hall, dripping with blood. The whole event deeply moves Percival although he does not understand. As he has learned earlier, he does not ask questions about what has happened.

After a night's sleep he can find no one in the castle anymore to talk to about what happened.

Percival only finds his horse and leaves the castle. The drawbridge closes after he has passed. Percival continues on his way and has many adventures, coming ever closer to King Arthurs castle. Then he sits on his horse and sees three drops of blood in the snow. This puts Percival in a trance and he can look back on his whole life. He then meets two knights who want to fight with him. After a long and exhausting battle he vanquishes them both. When he wakes up, he is invited by Gawain to enter the castle he had seen from a distance: the castle of King Arthur. There, an ugly woman offends him. She blames him for not having asked the question concerning King Amfortas's wounds. Finally, Percival feels the desire to know and hence to ask questions. He leaves Arthur's castle in search of the Grail Castle. After many more adventures and almost total desperation, he finds the Grail Castle for a second time. He can enter the castle and again there are strange events observed by Percival. He again meets King Amfortas and asks him the question: "Uncle, what art thou suffering from?"

By this question the healing process of King Amfortas commences and it is also the beginning of the process of Percival becoming the Grail King.

The whole legend you will find described in the wonderful "Percival" story by Wolfram von Eschenbach. It shows us the story of the educational path towards the horizontal self-leadership of modern man. We know little or nothing at the outset and we have to go a long way of questioning what we observe and trying to make sense out of it for ourselves, before we can even start to understand how the social reality works around us. We can have the courage to explore the open space we find and to use the potential of the free exploration of this open space to strengthen our leadership. This requires us to take responsibility for our life and for the community we are in and are a part of. It gives us the perspective needed to become wise and do good. We all can participate in the process of leadership and follow this path.

A leadership experience: 45+

"Till 21 you learn, till 42 you battle, till 63 you become wise and after 63 everything is a gift to you."

The demographic development of the population in Germany's society has recently gained enormous attention. The drastic effect on the social security system of the so-called "ageing society" and the diminishing birth rate is a real concern both in politics and society.

For the Sparkassen Magazine, this subject is an up-to-date theme as well. *"As a major employer in the area and an important regional bank, we have to think the consequences of this development through now and make according provisions,"* comments one of the bank's directors.

Presently we have roughly 850 employees in the Sparkasse over the age of 45. Let's simply call this group "45+". If we include the prospect of our staff having to work till the age of 67 in the future and that employees are allowed to work part-time, we have to assume that the number of 45+ employees will grow from 38% today to 55% in 2020.

2005	2010	2015	2020
37.8 %	49.5 %	54.1 %	55.1 %

What shall we do? The need for a concept for 45+ is clear.

As one of the first Sparkassen in Germany we decided to dedicate ourselves to this issue and to come up with an answer. Project 45+ was born. What started out as a working title for the project became quickly a well-known brand name throughout the organization. This project 45+ was at first taken up by the HR department and was driven by three of their members. After a number of interviews with our staff, it became rapidly clear that younger and older employees have very different motifs when at work. The requirements and challenges for older employees were obviously of a different kind than for the younger ones. However, it also transpired that a concept "45+" should not be a fixed concept, but instead should create space for each individual employee to explore their own thoughts for their own further development. This direction of thought had been the result of our interviews with our older colleagues, which had soon uncovered that there was no real "typical" older employee and a single one concept for their development would not be enough.

Conclusion: The "project" 45+ was transformed into the "process" 45+.

This process 45+ was not only totally new to our company but also to the wider Sparkassen community. For the first time we started feeding off individual initiatives, personal experience and the richness of ideas of our 45+ employees, including their requirements and wishes into the process.

What does this mean? What was the goal we wanted to reach with this process?

We have designed a very basic principle for this process:

The concept 45+ is based on the respect we hold for our employees. Participating in the process creates chances for them and for the Sparkasse. The employee allowed the free space needed to take steps according to his or her personal motivation and needs.

It was not our intention to follow the classical career path, like we would pursue for the younger staff members; the process is aimed at creating the opportunity for the next individual step in an elder person's life, also taking the conditions of their present job into account.

The launch event, June 2007

On the 15th of June we officially started the process 45+, which would run for the next six months. Sparkassen directors invited a total of 40 employees from the 45+ group to participate. They came from different departments and positions in the bank. After the general director had made the first introductory remarks and the bank's HR manager gave the first introduction on the process, I elaborated on the different biographical life phases, human learning and development within the company context: *"We do not only learn in the class room but also through dialogue with other people. We reflect and dialogue. Learning is based on an inner responsibility. Learning is stimulated by participating in small learning groups. We read, study, research and experiment, and this we do together without the restrictions from a hierarchical distance. The human being is placed in the center. We dialogue in a horizontal way. We do not always need to look for grand solutions, but we make small steps in the process instead."*

Each participant in the process was handed the task to reflect the following question: *"What is my next personal step in my life and what is the next step for the Sparkasse?"*

This question was all the participants offered as guidance at the beginning. This approach was unusual and innovative to them. Each one had to find their individual access to the process.

This process is about "the inner career". To start moving mentally to realize the new options in my present job as well, that is what this process 45+ is about.

The group of 40 was divided into two groups of twenty employees each and each group in turn nominated two process owners to help the group in making the process evolve. The process owners then assisted the groups to subdivide again into smaller syndicates of five. These small syndicates reconvened at several occasions over the following half year. The syndicate meetings allowed the participants to share experiences and learn from each other.

The interim meeting after three months
A "halfway" meeting was held after three months, in which each participant presented their ideas and outlined their next steps; how they were working on the details of these next steps and where they expected to be after the half-year period. They openly shared their experiences in this process with each other, their anxieties and expectations.

The final presentations after half a year
All participants presented their results to each other and to two directors of the board at the end of the full period of the six months.

All group members displayed an extremely high level of enthusiasm and motivation, presenting quite some surprising results. They had explored a whole range of suggestions, like: "PC training for elder employees", "Specialized senior consultants for senior clients", "How to stay fit at work", "Meetings for senior employees", "Coaching your younger colleagues", "Effective work processes", "Team development for customer process improvements".

Some of the presentations were made with a creative flourish, with the use of drawings, PowerPoint presentations, painted pictures or symbols like a tennis ball or a special doll. One presentation was even held without the use of words.

The processes themselves, however, had not been fully completed. All participants were fully committed to implementing the experimental results in their day-to-day work processes. This proves that it was not about developing ideas for others to implement, but that the group members felt a strong sense of ownership for their results and it was actually about realizing their own ideas, which could also benefit others.

Conclusion: *"Small deeds that one does are better then big deeds that are only planned."* (G. Marshall)

The process has in any event confirmed that both personal and company development can rely and be built successfully on experienced employees themselves.

Marie-José (participant): *In June 2007, I was invited by my line manger to participate in "45+". Initially, the idea in itself almost gave me nightmares: "What is this all about, what is being expected of me?" I kept asking myself. After the first introductory meeting, the panic and nervousness had subsided, but I still did not really know what my input to the group could be. In our first syndicate group meeting, I was relieved to see that the others had the same problem in finding their own theme, but this changed relatively quickly. Our process owner tried to explain to us how we could work together and progress in this syndicate. I soon found my theme: "Consulting foundations by a seasoned and experienced employee". Once back in our branch office, I started this extra work and I got very good feedback. When I now sleep badly, it is due to the excitement in me doing more work to further progress this subject."*

Ursula (participant): *When I started the "45+" process, I was very insecure; how should I contribute to the process and what should my theme be? This was a completely new and unusual work experience for me. When I now look back, I view the whole process as very lively, exciting and invigorating. It was a good opportunity for me to initiate some changes in the company, to get a broader perspective on things and enlarge my scope of activity. It was something totally different from the normal work I do. I developed a sense for very different aspects. Working together in the syndicate group I found very constructive and we also had quite some fun together. It actually made me happy.*

Gerlinde (participant): *When I was asked to participate, it came as a shock to me: "Why me?" Now I can say that I needed this little push to discover new challenges. I now see this as a valuable experience for me and I took up my theme with growing confidence. After implementing my theme, "Creative workshops by 45+ employees for 45+ clients", I was really proud of myself. It proved to be relevant for our company. It offers both the client and us benefits: a real win-win situation!*

Franz (participant): *At the beginning I thought: finally, older employees are getting some more attention! I found this way of process working really good because you could work in a creative way on your own theme and put your own ideas to work. I was surprised to see that we had so many different themes and that my colleagues were brave enough to present them in so many creative ways. At the final meeting, I was asked to start with the first presentation, which I do not very often have to do in my normal work. It was exciting. Working with my customers is familiar to me. However, making a presentation is unfamiliar to me. I can now see clearer what it means to present one's ideas in public, and can be more tolerant listening to others presenting their idea in the open space.*

Ruth (process owner): *The general director convinced me to take on this role. I am in the "45+" group myself. After the first meeting, I received a lot of e-mails from participants about some of their first thoughts of this process. Thinking of the motto: "All good things are simple", we could transform their ideas into reality in the syndicates. I observed some interesting phenomena:*

It was exciting to see how each participant found their next step, everyone took the chance to start a personal project and contribute to the process, the final presentations showed their personal experience and results. There is no limit to the richness of ideas that people can have.

I enjoyed being in this role of process owner, having to guide the process. It was very interesting to observe which ideas the participants had developed and how they tried it out in practice. I am convinced that we have laid the right foundation to continue.

Wilfried (process owner): *I coached two groups in which the members themselves worked on a project about the basis of personal responsibility, creativity and critical loyalty. The first meeting showed the insecurity of the participants, but it also showed their curiosity how this process would evolve. In the course of our sessions, jointly creating, brain-storming and criticizing the suggestions, we also experienced a lot of humor and fun. One thing always led us to a heartfelt laugh: the sender and receiver phenomena. One of the participants would be invited to this process over the telephone. He could not fully grasp the content of the invitation. He heard things like: "This is very important for the board of directors"; also the person on the other end of the line was speaking of "45 Klos" (which means "toilets" in German). He found this very irritating. At a certain point during the phone call he plucked up his courage to ask, "Where exactly do our directors want them (the toilets) to be placed in the office?" Only then did it became clear to the other person that something had not been understood at all. We frequently had to laugh about this little anecdote. And there were many more of the sort! My personal conclusion is: if we did not have this process, we should invent it immediately. It is this experience in the personal and professional life of the employees that is the golden capital, with which we are able to innovate creatively. I am convinced that this sort of process will offer the Sparkasse a lot of benefit—both for the clients and for the employees. It creates the opportunity to work with joy when being an older employee.*

Uta (HR department coach): *To set up and guide through a process from beginning to end was something entirely new to me. We have never done something like this ourselves and also other Sparkassen have not had this kind of experience. I was very curious to see how it would work. When I listened to the final presentations, I was impressed by the many ideas of our "45+" employees and I really enjoyed the many different ways the final results were presented. It was very satisfying to see how the participants had mastered the challenge as this is not their daily routine.*

CHAPTER 9: The human creation

1. The paradox world

In this last chapter, I will try to evaluate the whole content of this book at a more philosophical level. This can be helpful in the process of internalizing the key ideas presented in this book in one's own leadership thinking, doing and being. It can broaden and deepen our personal view on man and organization and the meaning of the leadership process for developing and changing ourselves and our organization.

1.1. The natural and the organized context

It is not only that we today live in the beautiful creation of nature and cosmos, a creation that gives us all the resources for our lives, but we also increasingly live in a world of our own creation, embedded in the modern organization. We are living, in this sense, two lives at the same time. We are part of the natural world; our body and spirit are intertwined with the streams of life. We are also part of the continuous effort of shaping and maintaining our own world, the world of technology, systems and work processes.

What I find striking is that the key values and meanings underlying our lives in the natural and cosmic contexts are expressed in a special language—like: "we love another person", "we respect the soul of another being", "we experience the blessings of life", "we suffer the failures and punishments of our mistakes"—a language that is totally absent in the organized context which we have created ourselves. In this context we have developed a totally different language, such as: "aims that we want to achieve", "profits that we want to make", "the management of our efforts", "structures and techniques to produce", "financial steering and cost management".

This difference in language and underlying values and beliefs may be an expression of the many barriers we have created, both within and outside ourselves, in introducing the most important values of human life, such as freedom, love and respect, into the organizational context. It is not easy in the organizational life to stand up for your own beliefs, your inner convictions, your dreams and hopes. The paradox of this is that we have a strong inner longing to create valuable life in our own creations, but at the same time we do everything to keep this separate from our personal life in the natural and cosmic context.

1.2. The paradox of the soul

The key expression of this paradox is the experience that it is not self-evident to use the word "soul" in the organizational context. Does the organization, the human creation have a soul, and how is the individual soul connected to the soul of an organization? As I have noticed, this question arouses a strong resistance and contradiction with many people. They find it offensive to use such language and thinking in an organizational context. "Do not offend my inner beliefs," they say to me or, "This is just wishful thinking and has nothing to do with the rational and functional structure of an organization."

However, I believe this might be exactly the *right* moment to address this question!

Why do I think so?

In organizations we see a growing tendency that people express an inner need to come closer to a sense and an intrinsical understanding of what they are doing there. There is a growing movement, for instance, to ask why we are destroying nature and the climate with our organized industrial efforts, why we are not choosing a durable and sustainable way of life, how we could be more conscious of the connection between people, planet and profit, how we might safeguard the future of our children, how we are going to handle the expected disasters of climate change, people migration, pollution, aggression against each other, and the stress and pressures of our technological life.

1.3. Disintegrating communities

The traditional structures of society, such as religious communities, regional population structures and even family life, are rapidly disintegrating to the point where we have little time left for each other or for taking the opportunity to reflect on what is happening, how it influences our lives and how we can connect to the deep roots of our lives and the life of the communities we belong to. Our Sunday no longer serves to reflect on the sense of life and death. We have no breaks anymore in our professional life to regain strength and consciousness of what we are doing and the next steps we need to take. Parents have no time to raise their children, responsible leaders have no time for their staff. Individuals have no time for prayer, for joining ceremonies of mystic initiations, for seeing friends and sharing the values of life or even going to the funeral of a relative.

So it might be a good moment to reintroduce the question of the human soul in relation to organized life and to explore the meaning of connecting our personal life values to the values of the organizations we are participating in.

2. The human soul

The creation we meet in life—nature, cosmos—is harmonic in itself. By harmonic I mean that in natural creation everything stands in a stable and reliable relationship to everything else.

Sun, moon and earth follow their path in the cosmos.

A plant grows, the air is there. Our spirit and body are embedded in this harmony. Our heart beats and we live our life every day. We are able to enter into the world of creative forces, which shape and maintain this wonderful natural and cosmic world. We can be initiated into these worlds and we can find a personal relationship to the natural and cosmic world.

I see science as a way to achieve that. In our quest for knowledge through natural science, we try to discover the laws working in nature. We have made substantial discoveries—at an ever-accelerating pace—on how the natural world is made up and how it maintains itself. We have analyzed this natural world, put it on the platform of our research, and we have documented the gained insights so that new generations can build on them.

But it is not only science we use to explore the world. We have also developed the arts to explore this most mysterious of worlds. We have reproduced the world we find when we are born; through the arts we have tried to show the forces at work in these worlds. Through music, painting, architecture etc. we have expressed how we see this world and how this world sees us. It is a dynamic, ever-evolving way of relating to the natural and cosmic world and we have placed into that world the human being as the center of its existence. A long time ago, the arts were far more connected to our religious interaction with this unknown world of creation and existence. We have seen the gods at work in this creation. We have seen the angels and archangels living in the invisible world, by which our observable world is created. We have found many ways of believing, of communicating with these worlds, and we have expressed this in a fantastic variety of rituals and community celebrations of this unseen life.

The basic root of exploring these worlds in these ways is the fundamental idea that it all exists in an organic togetherness. We can analyze, we can differentiate, we can explore its various parts—but ultimately we end up in wonder at how it all stands together, relates and communicates.

2.1. The individual consciousness

Through the many ages of research and exploration of this world with our growing consciousness, there is one question that has remained unanswered and which is key to the Sense-Making of our exploration. It is the question of how the human being has come to the individualized consciousness we see today. Other than plants and animals and stars, we seem to have an individual consciousness, which enables us to stand up on our own feet, in our own perception of reality, in our own biography. This is the question of the human soul and how the soul relates to everything else that there is.

This human soul manifests itself on earth in our individual ego and this individual ego makes itself, out of its own nature, known in our thinking, feeling, willing. These are the three manifestations of the human soul. Let me give a short description of these different manifestations of the human soul.

2.2. The individualized soul: thinking

Our individualized ego as soul is able to observe images and create them. In our body we have an array of senses enabling us to observe. These senses, such as touching, smelling, seeing, hearing, but also senses like finding equilibrium, experiencing life forces, exploring language, enable us to connect to the realities we experience. It is the individualized connection we can make with reality. These senses can be trained to function in a highly perfected state, and this can enlarge our awareness of what is there and what we are meeting. This is, however, not all: we can also add meaning to these observations and experiences by augmenting, from our free will, the language, meanings and ideas, lending an understanding to these observations. The thinking quality of our soul can embrace the observed realities we meet and give them a meaning, make them communicable. We can share images with others, and in doing so we can extend and strengthen the meaning and understanding.

2.3. The individualized soul: feeling

Our individualized ego as soul can also relate to everything it meets in feel-ings and emotions. Nothing we meet and observe and explore leaves us with-out a feeling or emotion arising from that meeting. In ourselves we make a "heart" connection and we feel the surge of emotions and longings, which follow either our embracing of reality or maintaining our distance to it. This is a fantastic ongoing process of bridging reality to our ego with these surfac-ing feelings that arise and which we can then share with others. We can be joined in this process and it gives us an enhanced relation to what is happen-ing around us. We can enter the world with our feelings in a compassionate and emphatic way; we can be animated by the world and the other people we encounter, and we can start to connect to them.

2.4. The individualized soul: willing

Our individual ego interacts as soul in the world we experience. We are not only a passive part of the world; we also grasp the world in our hands and start to transform it. We challenge the realities we encounter to show themselves, to open up and to share with us the forces and themes which are working in them. We transform nature into the goods we use and consume, we build our own homes and cars and telephones and live and work with them. We are on a never-ending path of changing the world into the technological being we spend so much of our time in today. It is a process of destruction but also of using, of constructing and building.

2.5. Breaking through boundaries

The significant consequences of this threefold manifestation of the soul of the human being are that we are moving towards a process of breaking through the natural boundaries we find in nature and cosmos. We are leaving the or-ganic and harmonic world and are entering the boundless world of liberated forces, previously kept in balance by organic processes. This could mean that we are no longer embedded in the godly hereditary we come from and are, in this sense, living in a godless world. This is confirmed by the observation that the worlds we have created can not regenerate themselves, unless the human being makes the effort for this world by maintaining it. But we can also see that the worlds we create have no direct sense of themselves and that we are the ones having to add the sense to this world. It means that these worlds will make sense in different ways to different individuals and there is no obvious and compelling common denominator for this between us.

So, through the actions of our individual ego as a soul in the world that is given to us, the natural and cosmic cohesion of this world is destroyed and as a result we live in a godless world. Aristotle already showed us this in his economic writings. We can also find this process described in the different records of the history of human development. We are living in two worlds that have fundamentally different bases of existence, and we see this expressed in the difference we can experience as living in the natural and cosmic world, compared to living in the organized world we have created ourselves.

2.6. The paradox existence

It is my opinion and vision that when the individual soul breaks through the natural and cosmic boundaries and touches and transforms this natural and cosmic cohesion into a human organized structure, then the harmonic cohesion changes into a paradoxical existence. All that man touches and transforms on earth changes into a contradictory way of existence. This is so because there is no inherent organic principle working in it any more, and it is only the human principle we ourselves have embedded in our constructions that is the source of its sense.

Instead of a harmonic world, we create a paradox world, a world that is in itself contradictory.

Our human creations are paradox creations; they exist in contradictory ways of being.

This is also shown by the fact that all we create is expressing itself in polarities, that is opposite forces. We create a world that is divided into under and upper, in inside and outside, in history and future, in expressing and understanding, in question and answer, in need and offer.

Nothing of our creation can exist out of itself, nothing of our creation has sense in itself other than the continuation and sense that we give it ourselves.

3. Constructing a house in Ireland

I have been a regular visitor of Ireland for many years. I stay with my relatives in a nice, old cottage my brothers bought some 32 years ago and which they have kept at quite a simple standard. It is positioned five kilometers outside a little village and it is embedded in a rural structure of little farms with a small community of widely spread families and individuals. The surrounding nature is beautiful and bustling with life.

Two years ago, I had the opportunity of buying a little piece of land on the other side of the river. It was the home ground of our next-door farmer, Pegoe Kennedy. It had been sold 25 years ago by his father and sister, but the owners never had used the cottage and land. So nature took over and gradually destroyed the little cottage with its thatched roof. This had saddened Pegoe, but he had not seen a way to change it. When I bought the piece, I started to rebuild the old cottage. The dream of Pegoe was that it would rise in its old glory, exactly like it had been before. Whilst keeping the basic outline of the cottage, I wanted to make it a little bigger and roomier. In a delicate process of dialogue and cooperation, we found a way to reconstruct the house and integrate the barn into it as an extra bedroom.

The key challenge in the whole process was for me to find the right balance between all the different aspects and sides to this rebuilding and reviving of an old human creation. It was a real soul exercise to communicate my wishes and feelings and ideas to those other people involved in the process. I found a builder who, by his nature, could understand this and helped to construct the actual cottage and space around it according to the drawings and contributions made on the basis of the dialogue with all involved. In a rhythmic process of meeting and observing the things that were done and of planning the next steps, this human creation came into the world and with it the different worlds of dreams and longings and hopes of those involved.

4. Take care and make sense

First in this process we experience natural creation and this creation is objective and true, it is self-evident. We could see how nature followed its own course and took the house and land and turned it back to its origins. Then the hand of man intervenes again in this process, interrupting the natural self-perpetuating processes going on by themselves, and rebuilds a new man-made house and surroundings, which from now on must be maintained and kept up in its artificial state by the people involved in living in it.

The existence and sense for what the human being has created is only going to be present when the human being makes his intentions clear and looks after his creation, which means he takes responsibility for the continuation of a self-created reality, takes care of the Sense-Making process in a self-created reality.

In this way the human being gets chained to his own creation, which speaks to him continuously the words:

 take care of me, keep me alive,
 give me sense

So there is a growing human, paradoxical world being created on earth. We live and work in this world and this world is challenging us all the time, demanding our attention and sapping our energy.

Let me give you a few more examples of how this humanly created world works between us.

It is not self-evident that a person also does what he says

Imagine the endless examples you can find in your own life on this theme! When you look at your own deeds, thoughts and feelings you experience, your actions do not always correspond to your speech. This is also often the case with leadership in organizations. It is said, for instance, that the company will explore new markets and will be active in creating innovations, but in their real actions you actually see a securing of financial profits, cost cutting as a result and the laying-off of personnel. It is an ongoing struggle for all of us to have our thoughts meet our deeds.

It is not self-evident that when one person speaks, the other one listens

We experience in our life many situations where we speak to a person and where we have the impression that we are not being understood or even listened to at all. That is frustrating and upsetting. But you can also imagine that other persons can have the same feeling speaking to you. It is not in itself natural that we understand each other, hear each other and listen to each other.

Listening is an art that can be learned by concentrating on the other person and by trying to move along with the other person and his thoughts, rather than being too consumed by what is going on inside of you. Dialoguing with each other is an essential art in creating something together. Each value that we create, each product or service comes about through the process of dialoguing. In that process, listening to each other is the essential element, and this is not only listening with the ears but listening with the whole person and with all our senses.

It is not self-evident that the finished house will maintain itself

We may have the luck in our life to have the opportunity to build a home. It is certainly a special experience when you have the chance to design the house and to construct it. It is a process which requires excellent cooperation with all parties involved. Many things can go wrong and you can end up with a house you wouldn't have chosen. Once it is finished, we have to take care of it. It is surprising how fast one has to start the process of maintaining and taking care of it. The natural corrosion, the attacks on different levels from the outside but also the inside, the continuous use of its facilities require that periodically things be repaired or renewed.

It is not self-evident that the created quality system works by itself

It is quite normal in organizations today to quite busily install a lot of systems. We have logistics systems, financial systems, human resource systems, management information systems and many more. It is the more recent creation of quality systems that has gained a lot of attention. A wave has gone through "Organization Land" to create quality systems, especially with a view to convincing the client to remain loyal and sometimes, however, devolving quality control costs onto the suppliers. The process of creating quality systems is often a complex one. Not only does it require a complex administrative process, in which all the details have to be documented and checked by experts, but also the practical effort to improve the actual processes to a quality standard that meets the client's requirements. ISO and other systems have been largely implemented in the western business world. However, installing a system does not necessarily mean it is going to work by itself. It needs the consistent attention of many people all the time to make the system work. Quality standards are often not kept under the pressures of daily life, documents are incomplete because there is information missing, we sometimes forget the standards and produce at random, and so on.

The written novel gets meaning by being read

A writer writes a book, which is then published and goes its own way. It finds readers to absorb the text presented. Then an interesting process happens: quite often the reader can read something totally different from what the writer meant to say. The reader brings his individual fantasy into play and makes his own interpretation of the story. There is a gap to be continuously bridged between the intentions of the writer and the reflections of the reader. This turns the process into a creative one. A special version of the book starts to grow in the public realm, it gets its own biography and creates its own reputation.

The hotel comes alive when there are guests

A hotel has been designed with specific ideas on what guests might appreciate. The rooms are decorated according to special themes, the guests can make their tea in their room, which they really appreciate, the food is nutritious and of excellent quality. But all this will only start to take effect when there are guests actually in the hotel. The process comes alive through the interaction between staff and guests. There is a variety of wants and desires from guests and there is a variety of abilities and temperaments in the staff. No situation is ever completely predictable; one never knows exactly how things will work out between staff and guests. This requires a continuous process of fine-tuning, constant adaptations to changing circumstances.

The service is delivered when it is paid for

When we go to a shop and buy our goods, in the end we have to pay. It is a natural process in our life, but looking at it closely, it is always something that is accompanied by a lot of personal interpretations, feelings, judgments. What we find fair or not, what we see as a good balance between price and value, what the consequence should be when the service does not meet our expectations, but we, nevertheless, have to pay the full price. It is a world of emotions and choices and appreciations, and often a lot of talk afterwards about what we think of it.

The car drives when I steer it

If we have a car, it does not mean it will drive by itself. We have to do it ourselves and—under some circumstances—this can be a risky affair. As drivers we always have to adapt to the situation we meet on the road. If it is foggy and we can't see ahead of us, then the process is going to be totally different to when it is a sunny day with an empty road in the middle of nowhere.

5. To co-create our processes

The conclusion can be drawn that everything we create as human beings does not have a continuous existence in itself and a sense of its own. The existence and continuation of it depends on us as creators and we have to add the sense to what we do in a constant way to make sure that it keeps its sense. This is something that does not happen automatically. Everyone has to be in the actual process to be able to do this. That there is, indeed, a process that is not, in its self, self-sustaining. We have to actively create and participate in the processes for this to happen. That is the great challenge we have in life today, the challenge to consciously co-create the processes in which our life evolves and in which it receives meaning. It is no longer sufficient that we are simply part of an organic process, in which we participate and experience sense. It is us ourselves who have to commence creating the life process and meeting others in doing this. We are experiencing, because of the numerous different processes we are involved in, a growing dependency on each other. This is a new phenomenon in humans history. For a long time, we have been embedded in the natural, traditional, organic world of our surrounding nature, the community, as it was given to us by our ancestors and in our own consciousness, as we found it in our inner world. We have been breaking through these barriers and we now find ourselves outside this organic reality and in the self-created inorganic and paradoxical, multiple reality. It is for this reason that the human soul is individualized and becomes the invisible embodiment in which we live. Our thinking, feeling and willing has become individualized, and it is only as a result of our own efforts that we are integrated and connected to the world around us, the material world we have created, the community we have organized and the consciousness that we have developed, falling out of the harmonic world.

The ultimate experience of this we find in the organizations, to which we are attached as customers or workers. Here we are confronted with the human creation in its purest version, the organization, and it forces us to take responsibility to maintain and develop it ourselves, to give our organized existence a sensible place and meaning in our life. Here, we are totally dependant on each other in a new way. We can overcome the traditional differences and although we still might differ in belief, knowledge, skills and so on, we can cooperate and co-create with everyone—even those we would not really care to face in the traditional community context.

Let us concentrate now on the process of organizing and how this works in the human soul.

6.   Organizing and reflecting

As a consequence of what I have described above, it is inevitable in this self-created world that we have to continuously perform two processes at the same time.

▪ The first process is *organizing*.

▪ The second process is *reflecting*.

6.1. Organizing

What do we mean by organizing?

With organizing we mean that we have to be connected to each other in a consistent and continuous way, while the following key elements also have to be taken care of:

1. We have to choose aims and means and match them to each other.
2. We have to take care of the conditions under which the process can take place. This involves:
   a. We have to find the right constellation of people to jointly work with.
   b. We have to develop a common vision of how it should be done.
   c. We have to install the work processes with which this is realized.

This process of organizing requires the use of resources we find present in nature and the cosmos, and at the same time all the competences and capacities we have developed as human beings. This means that the talents we have must be transformed into real human abilities. This means that we must invest the capital we were given or have acquired ourselves in the next steps we take, it means that we have to allocate time and completely focus on the issue we meet, it means that we apply our energy, we attach our hopes, we expect to gain life satisfaction, we want to create a personal future and we want the community to participate and benefit, too. There might be many other intentions we could have in creating our organized life together.

This process of organizing, however, fully absorbs our time. As we gradually grow older, we get totally absorbed by the organized life and we lose our natural connection to the natural and cosmic world. It requires a courageous move to allocate space and time and employ energy to reconnect to this world. This can be expressed in taking time out, to meditate and pray, to engage with one another on what the sense of it all is. By reflecting on the effects we have caused, we can try to find out whether these effects meet our dreams or maybe how they might threaten our existence. We can also experience how we can easily get completely sucked into organized life and that, as a result, we can feel empty inside. To compensate this danger, there is the need for a balancing process: the reflection process.

6.2. Reflecting

In the reflection process we regenerate our sources and abilities.
- We reflect on what we are doing and add sense to it.
- We relax, put the matter aside for a while and regenerate our energy sources.
- We meditate and pray for strength.
- This reflective process needs a conscious act of creation against the ongoing and imposed stream of actions.
- We search for peace, a quiet spot, we try to stop time.
- This gives us the opportunity for something that might reveal itself to us.
- In this reflective space it is also the higher "I", our authentic being, that can express itself in our ego as soul.

In the encounter with the higher "I" we evaluate our actions and deeds and we try to find the fruits, the learning points in our reflections on these actions. It helps us to give sense to our life and it also helps us in the process of judging the morality of our deeds; be they good or not. In this way, we create the conditions for our next steps and find the revived impulses and intentions for our deeds here on earth.

Hence, it is valuable to become aware that as an individual we are constantly connected to two processes:
1. The process of organizing, which is important for the maintenance of our own creation.

2.   The process of reflecting, in which we add sense to what we have created.

▓▓▓▓ **"We live our life forward and give it meaning backwards."**

7.   Learning

In our paradox world, we have to rely on our own efforts to master this world. The gaining of this mastery happens in the ultimate and most specific human process we have: the process of learning.

7.1. The master and the pupil

The process of learning is first of all a process of rising and falling. We learn by trial and error, by recognizing our mistakes and extracting meaning from these. By our striving efforts and struggle to create, again and again, a next step, we can walk on the path of gaining real consciousness.

▓▓▓▓ **From trainee—to professional—to master.**

The philosopher George Steiner describes this in a wonderful way in his book "Lessons of the Master": *"We face learning and teaching all the time today. But the relation that originated our knowledge and culture for centuries we almost forgot. The relation between the master and the pupil. This seemingly anachronistic relation is the foundation of all we mastered in art, literature, religion and philosophy. Sokrates and Plato, Jesus and his apostles, Tycho Brahe and Johannes Kepler, Edmund Husserl and Martin Heidegger: almost till today we see the line of great teachers that generated great pupils. Master and pupil did experience not seldom a tensioned relation in which it was not only about knowledge but also about power, trust and compassion. From this perspective the history of ideas gains an enormous dramatic quality.*

We are being confronted with the fact that the reality we meet is different from how we had pictured it beforehand. One's life evolves rarely in a straight line, in a predictable and logical way; it often holds surprises. It deviates from where we thought it might be going. What we intend to do might fail in the end and it does not meet the expectations we originally had. Learning is about becoming aware of this failure, to accept failure as a surprise we did not expect. Through our continuous efforts to face the realities as they appear and to reflect on their meaning ourselves, we are offered the opportunity to discover the forces working in this reality, which we would not have noticed before. The reality starts to speak to us, it gives us its message. It is up to us to listen to it and start a dialogue with it. This is the process where the master teaches the student.

7.2. The sacrifice

We can find a deep quality of learning in the sacrifices we make. We are not alone on this earth, but we are together with others. We depend on each other and we experience a growing interdependency in our organized, self-created world. We need each other. We find we are part of communities.

Andrei Tarkovski says it like this: *"The relationships between people today are becoming of a kind, in which one always expects the other to adapt, that they sacrifice themselves and contribute to our future, while oneself is not willing to participate and is fleeing the responsibility for what is happening in the world. There are a thousand reasons and excuses to think of avoiding this responsibility, to have one's selfish interest prevail over honorable and higher tasks. Only few people have the will or the courage to take themselves seriously and to accept responsibility for their life and their own soul. But what does it mean to sacrifice oneself for the common benefit? Is this not the tragic conflict between the individual and the community? If the responsibility is not based on inner conviction and someone grabs the right to decide destiny—of others, as well as his own—and to make this destiny superior to the individual vision of how one should take a role in the development of society, then we only widen the gap between the individual and the society. The spiritual will to sacrifice cannot be forced on others, but has to be a voluntary, natural and self-evident support for the other person."*

In the community we meet our counterpart. Being part of a community, it is our own actions which might come across or even interfere with the actions of the other. Sometimes, I have to concede on my own actions and desires in order to create space for the other person. This opens a space within us, in which the true love for the other, the respect for the action the other is taking, can grow. It gives us the moral basis for our personal existence.
We can learn from our failures when we reflect on them and we can grow in posture as human beings when we are prepared to yield to the other person.

Making sacrifices as well as reflecting on our failures are paradoxical acts, but it is this paradoxical act which forms the moral quality of the soul and strengthens the development of the ego into an authentic personality.

7.3. The human consciousness

Through the process of learning and growing, we become more familiar with this paradox world and begin to understand how to build bridges between ourselves and the world around us. This leads to a growing consciousness, an awareness of what takes place.

This consciousness is the benefit of the work.

First of all, this new self-developed and individualized consciousness responds to the original development aspiration of humanity. It is the mission of humanity—and in it the individual being—to grow to a state of full consciousness with regard to the realities we meet and of our own being. The creator's act of creation, which also made man exist, is responded to in this way: "Each tree is known by its own fruit."

But this new consciousness also adds to the future creation. We are not only fulfilling the mission which was given to us, but we have also received the opportunity to add to the creator's world.

To understand this, we have to reflect on what is unique and specific in what the human being can contribute to creation.

To describe this world, I will concentrate on three values, which are specifically linked to the human being and to humanity. These forces play an important, decisive role in humanizing our organizational life.

I call these three human forces *love, freedom, respect.*

8. Love, freedom, respect

Love

We can learn to know and understand our creations and creator. Through the force of love we can connect our ego as soul to our work and our companions. Through love we find a personal, conscious relationship to the other person as well as to the caring world of forces that work behind it. With our love we can warm our creations, we can give them sense and meaning by connecting our destiny with them.

Freedom

The deeds that we do and the results they produce can be born out of freedom. We can, out of our free will, associate ourselves to goodness, to the truth and the beauty our ego knows, the golden fit of the human soul. This is not born out of our natural being but out of a consciously realized idea, the fine desire to want to respond to the ultimate human ideal: the spirit consciously acting out of our own free will. The authentic "I" chooses to do that.

Respect

We can create the bridge to all other worlds by meeting these worlds with respect. This means that we do not conquer or suppress these worlds, but rather that we enable ourselves to live in a creative relationship with these worlds, these beings.

We respect the being different of the other ones and we meet them.

"You are so beautifully different."

9. Stories of humanity

In our search to understand our human creation we can link to and read well-known stories of humanity. They are the ultimate expression of our developing process as human beings. A fundamental example of this could be the appearance and workings of the *Old* and *New Testament,* which have had such a great influence in many cultures in the world.

In the *Old Testament* the creation of man is pictured and described. The human being, having been born into a natural creation, breaks through the boundaries of good and bad and falls out of the natural order. He falls out of the harmonic world and arrives in the desert. A process then evolves in which God's creation, the human being, loses the connection to its roots. He is cut off from the harmonic world and arrives in the paradoxical and artificial human world. The search for the source then begins. Prophets and "learned men" show the community the way back to the origin. The community starts the journey to find its roots.

This process still happens again and again in a cyclical way. Nowadays, we also lose our origin, live our existence and attempt to reconnect.

In the *New Testament* this process is reversed in a decisive way. God's son, Jesus Christ, incarnates in a human existence and opens up the road for us all to the spiritual world of the Father. Through sacrifice, suffering, death and resurrection, the human being finds his way as an individual conscious being. This road leads through the community. This community is no longer only God's chosen people, but it is the self-created karmic constellation of people we create ourselves. Based on shared spiritual ideals, meetings and common striving, the human spiritual community develops itself. The Holy Spirit, which works in this, guides the human being in his striving process towards a godly existence.

Through this process, man returns to the spiritual world of creation, but now as a conscious being that dresses itself in freedom, love and respect.

This is man's gift to the spiritual world of creation.

10. Consequences

On the basis of what I have posted here, I would now like to describe the consequences of this view.

First of all, I would like to state that this image of the human creation and the organization, as the ultimate integration of all we have been able to create ourselves, leads to a reconsidering of what the guiding principles are, which we attribute to organizations.

In the modern western society, "organization" has a dominant functional connotation. It is seen as an apparatus that helps us to work with and shape our products and services. It is a target-oriented organism that, as a complex mix of processes controlled by systems, needs to be constantly maintained and refreshed by us to keep on performing smoothly.

However, in my view the organization is a life category in which, since many of us spend most our life in organizations, we achieve our aims in life. The organization is not only (1) a functional organism that produces but also (2) a living community of people that cooperate and live together as well as (3) being a learning experience for everyone involved and shaping one's personality. I see these three dimensions also as three valuable aims for an organization itself.

An organization can be an organism of high quality, in which human beings can accomplish some of their most intimate personal aims, where we can meet and find our karmic companions in life. However, it can also be a prison for the people involved, a destructive organism that ruins our life and leads us into the worst conflicts one can imagine. This aspect has far-reaching consequences for the way we deal with organizations. It means that we have the moral opportunity to value our life and that of others by shaping humanistic organizations.

This is about putting the relationship between the individual and the community at the heart of our efforts and our Sense-Making reflections. We can master this relationship by the help of three key concepts:

Life as a process

Dialogue

Biography

Life as a process

The first concept is *the concept of life as a process.* One can say that our life is embedded in the processes we are in. However, we still have little pertinent realization of what processes we are in and how we can handle these processes. In our personal life, we have created processes like working, studying, family life, making music, going on holiday, meeting friends etc. These processes we have given a rhythm in life, we have chosen certain contexts to handle the process, we communicate with others in the process, and we meet thresholds and resistance in the process. It is a cycle of events, for which we can take responsibility, and maybe in the most important ones we take the responsibility to advance the process further and rise through this to a higher conscious state of living. It is an art in life not to confuse these processes we are in too much. They have their own dimensions and characteristics as well as their difficulties. We tend to mix these processes and their problems up and in doing so can create disasters in life.

Organizations are also a complex mix of processes. There are production processes, logistic processes, financial processes, human resource processes, et cetera. These processes have their own dimensions, their own knowledge and rhythm, their own requirements, their own systems to control. These processes interact with each other through the people and teams dealing with them. In the process with the customer, the organization integrates all the benefits of these different processes. It is here that we can see the value creation that has been generated; this is the proof of the pudding! In an organization it is the leadership process that makes the other processes interact with each other and people cooperate with each other. The leadership makes things happen and takes care that the resistances and problems are dealt with so that the process can flow and lead to its value creation.

Dialogue

The second concept is *the concept of dialogue*. Processes flow horizontally between us and they can continue in the dialogue we have together. The basis for this is the principle *"that we help each other to make a step."* It is listening to each other that makes the thing work. It is helping each other to express oneself that creates a quality of life, the "substance" with which we can interact.

We are living in a chain of interactions, in which we cooperate and create value. It is in this chain that we also learn together on the basis of dialoguing about our common experiences and our reflections we have on them. It is in this dialogical chain that we meet people and start to understand how things work. In each step of the work process flow, the value of what people are doing is increased when they dialogue about how they see and understand the chain they are in and how the result of their work influences the work of others in the chain. In the chain, therefore, we not only see the transformation of goods and services to the point where they are purchased by the customer for consummation or use. We also see and experience the initiation of living communities, which together can make sense out of the basis on which they work and live. They are learning from experience and have the opportunity offered to them to improve the process together, to change and innovate it and to develop as professionals and as authentic human beings. We can achieve mastery, helping the next generations to make their steps and grow.

Biography

The third concept is *the concept of biography*. All organisms have a biography, write a life story. Reading personal biographies or biographies of organizations is always very interesting. Biographies are always a wonder of life; they are the unique expressions of an individual and what he can experience. The biography is the foundation for all Sense-Making, it is the backbone for our personal growth and maturing in life. Our biography is also the expression of who we are, it is the expression of how society has written itself into our life, and how ancestors and also next generations live throughout the personal biography. The biography is based on natural laws and rhythms or phases in life. We see growth as a child, coming of age, entering society, building up a personal network, facing crises and transformation, growing older, gaining wisdom or losing track and becoming bitter. Our biography is also based on the unique personality we have and it will start to shine through in the biography. Our biography can be a surprise even to ourselves, never having imagined at all that life would take this specific track or turn. Biographies of people get linked to each other through marriage, for instance, or through a life-long companionship or colleagueship. We grow into our personal biography by traveling to different kinds of work communities and life communities or even to idealistic or religious communities.

These three concepts can help us to understand and deepen the sense of organization. The consequence of this is that we can open up to the idea that organizations are not only functional, instrumental machines but also evolving, dynamic and learning communities.

Values and morals

If we can allow ourselves to create new and different images of organizations and of our organized life, we form the chance for key values and morals, which we experience in our personal life, to enter the organizational context. For instance, we can integrate the meaning of religion into working life in a wholly new way. We do not have to go to a specific religious community to experience religion in life, but we can integrate the religious inspirations we have into our work life.

We can connect, for instance, the meaning of "helping your brother" to our cooperation with our customer. It is not the selfish ego which tries to profit from the customer, but it is the authentic personality that meets the other, cooperates with him and learns from him.

We can connect, for instance, the process of taking initiatives in organizations with the personal development processes of following one's impulse, meeting resistance and finding the next step. It is a process of transition and rising to a higher level of consciousness.

We can connect the process of community building and leadership in the community to the personal ideal of being a servant to the aims others try to fulfill. It is less about me and more about the other.

We can live with the human values of freedom, love and respect in an organized world, which is there to serve each other and help each other to fulfill the mission of both the individual and the community. This will help balance and heal the ongoing process of using nature, cosmos and spirit to satisfy our great variety of needs.

Two opposite reactions

In the practice of organized life, experimenting with this vision of organization, of the individual and organized community life, one can observe two opposite reactions.

People can experience a feeling of relief and hope. It resonates with a deep need to integrate working life and the life of personal morality and values. There are also those who see this as being offensive to them. It threatens very deep and sensitive inner feelings about religious and spiritual experiences, which are now faced with the rational and technological life of the organization. These people want to keep these worlds of work and inner belief separate.

We have to respect both attitudes towards the themes I have addressed here.

It is my hope that we will find ways of bringing the outer world of organizations and the organized life closer to the inner world of moral values and feelings of belief and knowledge. This can bring the world and us closer to our roots. It can strengthen the moral challenge to take responsibility for the world and ourselves and open up a path for future generations to take steps in this direction.

Bibliography

- Beck, Ulrich – Risikogesellschaft. Auf dem Weg in eine andere Moderne. Frankfurt: Edition Suhrkamp, 1986
- Bekman, Adriaan – Adviseren in verandering. Assen: Van Gorcum, 2005
- Bekman, Adriaan – Bewogen organisaties. Assen: Van Gorcum, 1998
- Bekman, Adriaan – De organisatie als gemeenschap. Assen: Van Gorcum, 2001
- Bekman, Adriaan – Kernkwaliteiten van leidinggeven. Assen: Van Gorcum, 2004
- Bekman, Adriaan – Lebendige Organisationen. Lengerich: Pabst Publishers, 2003
- Boonstra, Jaap – Dynamics of organizational change and learning. Chichester: Wiley, 2004
- Bos, Lex – Oordeelsvorming in groepen. Wageningen: H. Veenman & Zn, 1974
- Boulding, Kenneth – General systems theory, the skeleton of science. New York: Management Science, 1956
- Chia, R. – Organizational analysis as deconstructive practices. New York: Walter de Gruyter, 1996
- Dick, Bob – What is action research? 1999. Available online at http://www.scu.edu.au/schools/gcm/ar/whatisar.html
- Drucker, Peter – The age of discontinuity. London: W. Heinemann Ltd., 1969
- Glaser, B. and A. Strauss – The discovery of grounded theory: strategies for qualitative research. San Francisco: 1967
- Gleick, J. – Chaos: Making a New Science. 1987
- Greuling, Heinz – Chaos ist nicht gleich Chaos. Available online at http://www.quarks.de/dyn/3871.phtml
- Guba, E.G. and Y.S. Lincoln: Fourth generation evaluation. London: Sage Publications, 1989
- Hosking, D. – "Change works: a Critical Construction". In: J.J. Boonstra (ed.) – Dynamics of organizational change and learning. Chichester: Wiley, 2004, p. 259–279
- Hosking, Dian Marie and I.E. Morley – A social psychology of organizing. London: Harvester Wheatsheaf, 1991
- Lammers, C.J. – Organisaties vergelijkenderwijs. Utrecht: Het Spectrum, 1987
- Lievegoed, Bernard – Organisaties in ontwikkeling. Rotterdam: Lemniscaat, 1974
- Mintzberg, Henry – Strategievorming als ambacht. Harvard College, 1987
- Mintzberg, Henry – Die strategische Planung. Aufstieg, Niedergang und Neubestimmung. München: Carl Hanser Verlag, 1995
- Mintzberg, Henry – Power in and around organizations. Englewood Cliffs: Prentice Hall, 1983

- Weick, K. and R. Quinn – Organizational change and development: Episodic and continuous changing. In: J.J. Boonstra (ed.) – Dynamics of organizational change and learning. Chichester: Wiley, 2004, p. 177–197
- Weick, Karl – Sense-Making in Organizations. London: Sage Publications Inc., 1995
- Zwart, Cees – Gericht veranderen van organisaties. Rotterdam: Lemniscaat, 1972

CV Adriaan Bekman

Prof. Dr. Adriaan Bekman (1947) is founder and director of IMO Institute for Man and Organisation Development.

He is also co-owner and former managing director of Innotiimi, a Finnish consulting and training group, and he is the president of Associazione Motiva in Italy.

Since May 2005, Adriaan Bekman is Professor at Stenden University in the Netherlands. He is a key note lecturer at the management center de Baak and the development institute for professionals SIOO.

For more than 35 years, he has worked in client organizations in different countries as a horizontal leader for change and organization development.

Adriaan Bekman worked for many years as senior consultant and managing director at the NPI in Zeist, Holland.

He worked eight years for Shell International after he studied sociology (1964–1968) at the Erasmus University in Rotterdam.

Adriaan Bekman wrote his thesis "Bewogen organisaties" (1998) and over the past 30 years has published many books and articles on themes such as developing man and organization, leadership and self management, consulting change and the organization as a developing community.

Contact information:

Frank van Borselenlaan 13
3703 BA Zeist
The Netherlands

bekman@het-imo.net
http://www.het-imo.net

Appendix 1

360° research on horizontal leadership: examples and questionnaires

In the context of our horizontal leadership research we use a questionnaire of 16 questions. For each key quality of horizontal leadership we use four questions that each show a specific aspect of these horizontal leadership qualities.

These four qualities are:
- Steering in work and development processes
- Coaching the learning process
- Inspiring with a vision
- Confronting and making interventions in the process

The 16 questions:

1) I make choices for my organization that make a difference
2) I learn from my companions
3) I can imagine the future and together with my employees go for it
4) I stop the process immediately when things do not work out
5) I support my employees by taking clear standpoints on critical issues
6) Listening is an art I really practice
7) I can inspire others to follow a challenging goal
8) I am not afraid to confront the other
9) I create optimal conditions for my employees to work in
10) I am always looking for the next development step for my unit
11) I love to dialogue with others on ideas that make sense for my unit
12) I am happy to set the boundaries
13) I create the process that make things happen
14) I stimulate others to make a learning step
15) I can stimulate the other to create a dream of the future
16) I am not afraid to cut projects

Participants score each question on a scale of

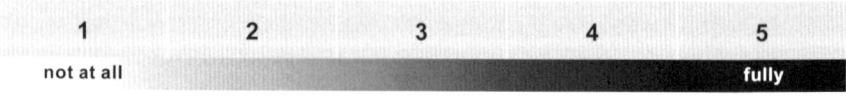

The scale for scoring

1 __	5 __	9 __	13 __	: add numbers = ____	divide through 4 = ____	Steering
2 __	6 __	10 __	14 __	: add numbers = ____	divide through 4 = ____	Coaching
3 __	7 __	11 __	15 __	: add numbers = ____	divide through 4 = ____	Inspiring
4 __	8 __	12 __	16 __	: add numbers = ____	divide through 4 = ____	Intervening

These questions are presented in a 360° analysis to the leader himself, four employees, two colleagues and the boss of the leader. The participants/respondents can calculate their scores themselves and give them to the leader. The leader can use a coaching dialogue with the process owner to interpret the results and the striking differences in how the others value the key qualities of this leader. The leader can start a dialogue with the others, preferably in a group dialogue. My vision is that if there is a greater difference than one point, it is worthwhile looking into this aspect. The best way to use the results is to see the four qualities in relation to each other. There is not one best way to which the leader can compare his score. It is more important to look into the differences of the different respondents and try to understand what this means for the leader's leadership practice.

An example
A leader scores 4.5 for coaching himself and this expresses his attention to this quality coaching of his workers in the learning process. The employees score 2.5, the colleagues score 3 and the boss scores 4.8. The leader can investigate the meaning of these different scores. It seems to be that there are differences in views on quality. One can go into more detail looking at the four questions on coaching. Through dialoguing with the others the leader can find out what created the differences in opinion. This can lead to a specific intention by the leader and helps him to come to a next development step in his horizontal leadership.

The practice shows the fruitfulness of this research for individual leaders, particularly when it is done in the context of an organizational development process in the company.

We will illustrate this with two cases.

The results of a pharmaceutical company

In a pharmaceutical company the team leaders and department heads research their horizontal leadership qualities. After they have analyzed the results individually, they have spoken together about the results, how to interpret them and what could be the next step in developing these qualities. Four scores of four leaders illustrate the kind of picture they see.

	LR 1	CO	WO	BO	LR 2	CO	WO	BO
Steering	3.25	4.25	3.8	3.75	4.0	4.25	3.9	4.5
Coaching	3.75	4.5	3.5	3.5	3.75	3.75	3.5	5.0
Inspiring	3.75	4.0	3.4	3.5	4.5	4.0	3.5	4.5
Intervening	3.0	4.1	3.5	3.75	2.75	4.0	3.75	4.25

	LR 3	CO	WO	BO	LR 4	CO	WO	BO
Steering	3.5	4.4	4.4	3.75	3.75	4.5	3.9	4.0
Coaching	3.75	4.5	4.5	4.0	3.75	4.75	4.0	4.75
Inspiring	4.25	3.9	4.1	4.0	3.75	4.25	4.6	4.25
Intervening	3.75	5	4.0	2.75	3.25	3.75	3.4	4.25

LR = leader   CO = colleague   WO = workers   BO = boss

In the dialoguing between one leader and his respondents it was observed that the leader had a more positive view on his qualities than the workers of this leader. In another case, the leader saw himself as steering and inspiring but not really intervening, while the workers responded in the opposite way.

The results of a leadership research process in a Brazilian agricultural company

	LR	WO	LR	WO	LR	WO
Steering	3.75	4.1	4.0	4.0	3.75	4.25
Coaching	4.0	3.5	3.25	3.75	3.25	4.4
Inspiring	3.5	4.5	3.25	4.25	3.0	4.0
Intervening	2.75	4.5	2.0	4.5	3.25	4.4

	LR	WO	LR	WO	LR	WO	LR	WO
Steering	4.0	4.0	3.75	3.75	3.5	4.25	3.25	4.0
Coaching	4.5	4.75	3.25	3.75	3.5	4.5	3.75	4.5
Inspiring	4.25	5.0	3.25	3.75	3.25	4.5	3.5	4.25
Intervening	3.25	4.5	2.75	4.0	2.25	4.25	2.75	4.0

LR = leader   WO = workers

In this organization, it was striking for the directors to see that they had scored the key qualities less strongly than the co-workers had scored them. Intervening was something they did not like to do, but the workers saw them as strong on this point.

The use of these 360° analyses is stronger when it is integrated in a research and development program in which leaders try to figure out how their horizontal leadership is working and how they can improve the leadership qualities and balance them in the right way. It can be, for instance, that the intervening is too strong and combined with little coaching of the workers. This could be better balanced. The leaders can explore the horizontal leadership space and expand their repertoire for working in that space.

Appendix 2

The horizontal leadership methodology

During many years, we have explored the different ways of making the leadership issue clearer and more transparent. How is leadership and—in particular—how is *horizontal* leadership working and how can we get a deeper insight into the dynamics of horizontal leadership? This research has yielded the insights in the inner mechanisms of leadership in organizations, as I have described them in this book. Here we come to the methodology that I have been publishing in the Dutch Scientific Magazine 'Management en Organisatie'. It gives us the theoretical basis for the further exploration of the horizontal leadership question and our fundamental reflections on this.

1. Different types of methodology

In the course of the last decades, we have first of all explored four relevant scientific methodologies giving us the epistemological starting points for developing a specific leadership methodology and enabling us to explore the leadership question. We will shortly characterize these four methodologies that have given us a foundation for exploring the leadership question in a new light and that we have used as sources. They are:

Action research methodology

Social constructivism methodology

Chaos theory methodology

Developmental theory methodology

1.1. Action research methodology

We have seen the rise of the action research methodology during the second half of the last century. In action research we discovered that it does not make sense to try and understand social reality in an objective way because we always influence and change the social reality by whatever intervention we do.

During the seventies, the action research methodology looked for a new way of doing social research. Action research can be described as: *"a family of research methodologies which pursue action (or change) and research (or understanding) at the same time. In most of its forms this is done by:*

- *using a cyclic or spiral process which alternates between action and critical reflection and is*
- *continuously refining its methods, data and interpretation in the light of the understanding developed in the earlier cycles.*

It is, thus, an emergent process, which takes shape as understanding increases; it is an iterative process which converges towards a better understanding of what happens. In most of its forms it is also participative (among other reasons, change is usually easier to achieve when those affected by the change are involved) and qualitative." (Dick, 1999)

1.2. Social constructivism methodology

A second, most interesting approach to researching social questions is constructivism. It is based on post-modern philosophical and sociological views. Scientists like Weick, Chia and van Dongen represent this school of thought. The essence of their thinking is that the individual perceives the social reality as an interactive reality. The key point, as I once heard van Dongen say, is *"who is what and what is who"*, which expresses the point that all is observed by human beings, however, individual observations of different people vary from each other and it is only afterwards that we are able to make interpretations, different interpretations of what has happened and what it means. The whole of the story is put together afterwards through interaction with each other. Chia concludes that traditional modernist science is *"downstream"*, it is researching in crystallized stream beds. He wants to see more *"upstream"* research, where the stream of events is unpredictable. Weick shows us that we cannot research objectively in social reality, while we are watching this reality evolve. Only afterwards we can recall from memory what we think has happened. Then we see that different observations and interpretations play a role with those people who were involved in the process.

Modern sciences are part of today's problems, say Ulrich Beck and Anthony Giddens. Science can no longer pretend to be objective and to make objective statements. Science can not be the protector of the truth and claim to make truthful generalizations. We can only learn through science by jointly reflecting on the findings with the help of a sound methodology.

1.3. Chaos theory methodology

Another interesting approach in our research has been the chaos theory.

Chaos theory has been further developed by scientists, who want to overcome the limits of cause-and-effect reasoning and objective/subjective standpoints underlying the empirical approach. Inspired by weather research, where it gets more difficult to predict the weather the longer the next period of prediction is to be, they found that there are, nevertheless, underlying patterns that can metamorphose into different patterns on the basis of very small interventions. This was expressed by the image of a butterfly in Japan which, by fluttering its wings and through a series of subsequent interactions with other movements, ends up in initiating a thunderstorm in the USA (*"Butterfly effect"*). We live with many simultaneous interactions and effects of deeds from various origins, which on the surface have an unpredictable character. In the aftermath, we can research the sequence of events, while beforehand we can only venture a prognosis of what might happen. Chaos theory methodology allows us to deal with complex, paradox social phenomena, which we do not have to reduce into manageable standards and repeatable interpretations. We do not have to exclude events which we are not able to interpret within any specific methodology. We can leave the social reality intact and learn to understand it.

1.4. Developmental Theory methodology

A fourth methodology we found useful is the developmental methodology introduced by Bernard Lievegoed (1964), Cees Zwart (1972) and Lex Bos (1974).

They developed a methodology that:

is used as a conceptual framework for clarifying as well as creating organizational development and change processes in organizations;

is based on an interactive developmental vision concerning human and social development processes, inspired by spiritual sciences;

is part of visionary and critical reflections on organizational and management practices as well as concepts like the ones developed by Peter Drucker (1969) and Henri Mintzberg (1987).

This methodology is appropriate for researching the organized community and its processes of development, change and innovation as they are handled by practitioners in organizations. This methodology uses the tension between the individual and the community as its foundation. It is the creating principle for social issues in our times of individualized consciousness and organized communities.

Bernard Lievegoed describes the essence of this methodology in his book "Organisaties in ontwikkeling, zicht op de toekomst" like this:

"In our conception of social development the key point is that a social organism is always 'on the move', coming from a specific past and moving into its own future.

The specific past is made out of 'choices made' that lead to institutions with concepts, values and motives that must be accepted as given facts. In its own future we find the freedom, the possible new choice of aims and policies.

The development of a social organism is always embedded in a bigger field. Each social system is a subsystem of a bigger system. The internal development is always influenced by concepts, values and motives that work as parameters on the individual system. Each social organism one must be viewed in the light of the surrounding 'culture'. Developmental action (social action) is thus a process with an internal and an external side. Not only is the social organism influenced by its surrounding culture, but this culture is also being influenced by the social system."

Bernard Lievegoed goes on to describe three characteristics of development:

Development is a discontinuous process, irreversibly moving in time, following the principle—the initial universal model of differentiation, integration—towards becoming a system of higher complexity.

Through development a "step by step, up the ladder" process emerges, in which older levels of subsystems might remain in existence, if dormant.

Through development a structure by levels emerges.

Bernard Lievegoed and his colleagues have described the developmental process of individuals and organizations in many variations. In it they see the sensible approach of our modern times to examine the human creation, which is the organization.

2. Key points

These four methodologies show us ways to research and improve our understanding of the mechanisms in leadership in today's social reality. They give us a new perspective for dealing with the leadership issue in the social reality.

These four methodologies have given us a methodological basis for developing our own way of researching the horizontal leadership process in organizations.

We will try here to formulate this basis in several short statements.

▨▨▨ Action and reflection go hand in hand. Horizontal leadership is a cyclic, dialogical process between people. During the process, our common understanding of what happened arises through our reflective interaction.

▨▨▨ However, we will only understand fully after the event. Persons involved will have differing observations and interpretations of what happened. Afterwards, we build our reality and give it sense in an interactive process.

▨▨▨ It is the leadership which stays close to the original source, where effects are unpredictable, that gains deeper insights into what actually happened. This requires a different leadership approach than the managerial approach we can use in downstream process streams with predictable results.

▨▨▨ Behind the observable but turbulent upstream reality, patterns are at work which are structuring seemingly chaotic phenomena.

▨▨▨ Understanding complex, paradox phenomena requires leadership not to analyze in an exclusive fashion, but rather to include during the process of understanding and interpreting.

▨▨▨ The leadership process is a cyclic process, in which we make "maps of understanding" together, which supports a continuous process. The leader is the designer of the process.

▨▨▨ We live with guiding principles, which direct our actions.

▨▨▨ Leadership issues and questions in the social reality require processes of development, change and innovation. These processes are by nature at the same time both reflective and initiating and they appear in organized contexts.

The individual and the organized community are contextual research frameworks that define the boundaries for the leadership process.

These key points have formed the foundation for the development of our own research framework, based on the horizontal leadership methodology that I will describe here.

3. Creating sense

I see the essence of our own horizontal leadership methodology primarily as a basis on which we can create and understand the Sense-Making process in organizations, and we do this within the organized community in the context of processes of organizational development and change. My basic assumption is that—in contrast to the natural creation, in which objectivity and truth are evidentially existent—in all that we as human beings create there is no self-evidence of existence and therefore no continuation of our creation by itself. We can observe this by the fact that all that we create as human beings will ultimately disappear again, either immediately or gradually, unless we look after it ourselves and maintain it. So we will also have to regularly make sense of all our creations, if there is going to be progress and continuity. In that respect, I see the organization as the ultimate human creation, in which the evidence for this creation can only be sustained through our ongoing maintenance and care by continuously adding adequate sense to it.

Processes of organizational development can mainly be seen as processes of creating this sense and continuity.

We do this by changing and by the innovation of our organizational structures, the cooperative constellations of people as well as our guiding principles. And for this we need a horizontal leadership process.

The horizontal leadership process methodology can be appropriate for this purpose.

4. Characteristics of the horizontal leadership process methodology

You will find here the seven characteristics of the horizontal leadership methodology. They are described in an abstract way and each characteristic is illustrated with a concrete example sometimes partly adapted from a story already described in previous chapters. To understand these characteristics, it is needed for each of them to meditate a bit on the description used, which at first might seem difficult to understand. The given example can help you to see the direction in which you can connect the characteristic to your own experience.

All characteristics can be seen as dimensions used by the leadership for understanding the change issue we have to tackle as well as dimensions for steering the change process in which the change issue is tackled in practice.

Characteristic 1: Reflection and action

The horizontal leadership process tackling change works through reflection and action, which means that the observed phenomena around the change issue are being interpreted after events that happened through a dialogue between those who were involved. The leader initiates this in networks of individuals and takes them through this reflective leadership process. The leader works in a dynamic and also always in a slightly different way by inviting new people to participate in the process and by sharing different interpretations of the effects of the observed events. This creates an interactive process with the people involved and it leads them to insights concerning the essentials of the change question or issue. Reflection and action as a process are combined in a rhythm created by the leadership.

To illustrate —————————————————————————————

In a bank, the general director wonders why the young co-workers show little initiative. He asks two process owners to investigate this. The two invite seven managers and interview them on the question. Only one of the seven can give a personal example of an initiative taken. She has inofficially given her young co-workers the responsibility to talk to those customers having passed a defined credit limit, something she did not like to do herself. To her surprise, this has had a very positive effect on the customers, her co-workers and herself.

The two process owners decide to create a company-wide process for young co-workers who will be allowed to take, individually or with another colleague, a valuable initiative forward, based on customer and company requirements for change. The young co-workers perform the whole process themselves and after half a year they report back, presenting the results to the general director, their line managers and the two process owners. This starts off a process in which all young co-workers—and there are several hundreds of them—are given this opportunity. More then 90% of them achieve valuable results in terms of customer satisfaction, company results and personal learning. They were able to involve their colleagues, to cooperate with them and to present the results to the management and the general director.

Characteristic 2: Cyclic sequence of events in time

The horizontal leadership process is reiterative. This means that "repetition" plays a central role in that the leadership questions the events that happened with a certain regularity. The happenings around the change issue unfold in a certain sequence. Past events in the change process are identified and analyzed by the leadership team in a reflective way and lessons are learned from this. Present events are researched in the here and now and are experienced as well as investigated in their actual sequence, and this can lead to further steering interventions of the leadership in the change process. Finally, future events are initiated by choices and leadership decisions that should lead to further and new steps, for instance in the form of new experiments.

To illustrate _____

A Rotterdam harbor company faces troubles around its general manager. The general manager is criticized by his governmental supervisory board for generally acting too independently and being difficult to control. Further investigation shows that this conflict of interest between the general manager and the governmental supervisory board had already occurred at certain intervals in the past, as it also had with their predecessors. The incident repeated itself frequently despite all the measures taken. A regular meeting of chairs would take place and each time the facts would be reported as breaking news in the daily newspaper.

The general manager reacts by initiating a cultural change process in his company. The company's employees and the governmental supervisor are involved in this process from the beginning. In the context of this process, the power position of the general manager is changed; a team of directors is installed, who share the power between them.

Characteristic 3: *Biography of man and organization*

The horizontal leadership that is dealing with the change process is faced with individuals in the process who contribute and make sense in the context of their own biography and the biography of the organization: it is about individuals and communities who are influenced by the change process that has an effect on their biography. In this biography of the individual and the organization, metamorphosis and growth are going on, which means that individuals and organizations are transformed over time to a higher level of consciousness. The leadership connects all it does in the change process to real people with real biographies as well as to the biography of the company to make understanding the change happen and to enable the right initiatives to be taken by the persons that are involved in the change process.

To illustrate

In a governmental service office, a manager describes her approach to leadership. It is her vision and position that, first and foremost, she should base her actions on her own uniqueness and meet the others also on this basis of the unique personality of each individual. She is always interested to hear from the other person his or her own vision and what the next steps are that will be taken. "I want to keep as many people on board as possible and to realize that I am willing to shape more space in goals to reach and roads to go on," she says. Some colleagues think she is a difficult person and she is stubborn. They tell her to exert more pressure on her people and show more "balls". "I only function well in a team, where variety is allowed," she says. "If that is not possible then they should not take me in." In time, more colleagues also chose to work out of their authentic being.

Characteristic 4: *Inspiring images*

The horizontal leadership process is inspired by stories that arise out of living, vital events, incidents, meetings, creative acts, confrontations and conflicts that happen in the change process. These stories that arise out of the change practice of people in the organization are shared and they start to live their own life. The stories can lead to further steps in the change process that individuals want to take. They also lead to the leadership stories that help new people to understand better what is aimed for in the change process. These stories are linked to views and concepts that the leadership uses for driving the change process. Thus, the community becomes sensitive to the issues and eager to ensure the continuity of the process.

To illustrate _____
A new organization resulted from a merger of two different, older organizations. After a while, top management becomes increasingly concerned about the integration of the two former organizational parts. There is the suggestion to use a video and help the co-workers to document their work processes and tape characteristic stories they have to tell as they experience them in their work environment. The resulting movie offers a wealth of images, which the community can look at and share together. The management also watches the movie and asks itself what the link might be between their policy stories, which they frequently communicate to staff, and the recounted work-process realities of co-workers shown in the films.

Characteristic 5: Convictions and leading principles

The events that happen in the change process are being interpreted by the leadership on the basis of their leading principles and convictions they carry in them. When unwanted events repeat themselves in the process, underlying destructive patterns in the organization are becoming visible. These underlying patterns are linked to the existing structures and systems being used. They can form the bottleneck for the change to take place The leadership has to tackle the deeper lying barriers in structure and also vision. They are going to look for new leading principles that could help to create new patterns and systems. This is expressed for instance in new mission statements, vision documents, strategic planning programs.

To illustrate _____
An organization grows quickly because of its fantastic products, which are sold in many countries around the world. The internal processes must be continuously adapted to accommodate the growth. This involves new production facilities, complex planning processes and changing labor conditions, but at the same time creates tension between co-workers. Each time something goes wrong, blame is sought at other doorsteps. The tension mounts and the general

manager has to intervene. In a specifically designed change process, the problematic interfaces between those departments needing to cooperate with each other most are examined and challenged by groups of co-workers themselves. As a result, some work processes are redesigned, for instance the process of developing and introducing new products. Co-workers come to realize that it is not always the other person who is the problem.

Characteristic 6: Observables and phenomena

The horizontal leadership connects during the change process to concrete phenomena and observables. It is about connecting the process to what is actually observable, the manifestation of what actually happened and what was created in social contexts. Phenomena are not only analyzed facts but first of all real-life experiences and observations of the people involved in the change process. The concrete context in which the change process takes place unfolds itself and the boundaries that limit the change process become more clear. Within this identified field of change, the phenomena are located and documented by the leadership.

To illustrate

In the meeting of the team, many issues are discussed. Participants start to notice that the same points tend to return. It is also observed that these points are only discussed in an abstract way. By doing it like this, each one of the participants comes to a different interpretation and the agreements that are made do not stick. When on occasion examples and facts are mentioned or described, the discussion becomes more concrete. Everybody understands better what is being discussed, although it also somehow generates embarrassment. When concrete examples are used and facts are mentioned, for instance, we see what the size of the issue is. Interaction improves and differences in interpretation become clearer, agreements become more concrete and, as a result, are better kept.

Characteristic 7: Empirical data

The horizontal leadership process works with empirical data because during the process the leadership checks with all those involved how they interpret the results of the change process and whether they find these results relevant.

This data clarifies the community's consciousness concerning the change issue during the change process and how it is experienced and observed by the community members.

To illustrate _____

Each year, the employees in this organization are asked about the issues for change they would like to see tackled. They discuss the question in groups. The issues that come up are transformed into questions and put into a questionnaire, to which everyone in the organization can contribute. Managers and co-workers all score the questions. Statistical data is fed back to them. Each team can see their own score as well as the score of the whole organization. Teams discuss the results and can decide to start initiatives and processes tackling issues which are seen to be important to act on.

These seven characteristics of the horizontal leadership process methodology become manifest and can be observed in the organizational development practice in an interrelated way as a consequence of leadership interventions in processes. In general, this happens in a fairly unconscious way. This methodology supports, however, the precise, creative handling by the leadership of organizational development and change processes. This increases the prospects that the leadership can approach the changing social reality in such a way that the leadership
  • does the community justice,
  • finds the point for the next intervention.

5. Application and ways to act

To experience the horizontal leadership process methodology, leadership has to actually apply it.

The *first opportunity* for leadership to act is by **continuously engaging with the social reality,** as this reality is created by ourselves.

The *second opportunity* for the leadership to act is by **changing work processes** as they are designed and performed by people in real working environments.

The *third opportunity* for the leadership to act is in **making conscious the guiding principles** as they operate in people's work. Which guiding principles direct people's thoughts and actions?

Continuous dialogue, changing work processes and making the guiding principles explicit I see as the key points for the leadership to concentrate on during the process of researching and initiating development, change, and innovation processes.

Opportunity to act 1: *Creating dialogue in the social reality*

The leadership becomes conscious of the question in their social reality by communicating to others. The way to leadership experience and observing the social reality is by questioning and exploring it.

The dialogue with the other and "exploring the question together" brings the leadership "inside the question".

Now it is important to do this questioning with a methodological consciousness. The leadership can do this using a dialogical approach.

The dialogical approach

The employee informs the leader about a question or issue that appears in his workplace / work process. The worker wants to clarify the point. The leader asks the employee questions helping the worker to describe the question/issue more clearly. This requires actual examples described by the employee in creating an image of what might be the issue. The employee also explores with the leader how he is related to the issue and what role does the question play in the biography of the employee and his organization. Together they try to identify the employee's next step in dealing with the question/issue.

The aim of the leader's questioning is not "to understand what the issue means for himself," but it is "to help his co-worker to better define the issue." The leader concentrates on how the employee describes the issue and what importance this issue has for him. This brings the employee into the position of confronting himself with the question/issue and gets a clearer view of it. The effect is that the question changes and that the employee now sees new opportunities to act.

An essential quality for dialoguing in this way is the listening capacity. To strengthen the listening quality, the leader can listen on three levels to his employee.

The *first level* is **following the employee**. What is he saying? This requires concentration.

The *second level* is **sensing**. What does this mean for the employee? This requires a lot of empathy!

The *third level* is **discovering the "intentional direction"** of the employee. Does he see a next step to make? This requires courage.

By listening like this, an inner space is opened in the employee by the leader in which the employee can express him/herself.

The social reality around an issue becomes meaningful when those involved engage with each other, when the issue is connected to the biography of the people and organization involved, and when they continue the process together, making steps and reflecting on the workings of these steps.

Opportunity to act 2: The researching and changing of work processes

The leadership researches the work processes and applies interventions through which the work process changes.

The work process flow, the result of the work process and the actual activities in the work process are the observables of an organization in action in which people create social realities by changing and innovating them. These observables give the material for the question being researched.

People do work processes and change work processes while doing the work process. They do this for instance with viewpoints like:

- The work process is directed to customers' needs.
- There is flow in the work process.
- Waste is minimized.
- We create quality and cooperate together.

People in the work process themselves research the process and change it. To be able to do this, the leadership can use the method described below.

Work process analyses

The leadership and a group of co-workers chose a work process that is not running smoothly. They identify who is the customer of this work process. Who is the one that uses the results of this work process?

They analyze the work process on three levels:

1st level: What is the sequence of activities of this work process, starting with the customer?

2nd level: What are the constellations of people collaborating in each work process activity?

3rd level: Who is the decision maker, who is responsible?

After the group has visualized the work process on these three levels, they identify the red spots in it. Red spots mean structural disconnections/bottlenecks in the work process that are observable and can be improved. This should lead to better customer service, a better flow, better cooperation and less waste.

For each red point the group can work out the critical idea for changing it. They select the best opportunities and start experimenting with the improvements in practice.

By doing this research and improvement process, the leadership and the people involved in the process can improve the interaction with the customer and the work process reality and as a result create an intensive, responsible way of dealing with this.

Opportunity to act 3: *Discovering steering convictions in our inner world that direct behavior*

The leadership researches their inner world and how this inner world is connected to the social reality that is created. Values and norms, convictions and ideologies work in the leadership and they show themselves in guiding principles. These guiding principles direct actions and behavior in the community in a real-life situation and they give it sense.

To be able to influence actions and behavior, the leadership must identify the guiding principles and let them become effective. The leadership can do this through integrating new ideas in their inner life and by gaining experiences in situations unbeknownst to them. The leadership can respond to these situations through various behavior patterns and actions. This gives the leadership and the community an opportunity to act in a new and different way in the social reality and also to see this reality in a different way than before.

The leadership can use an approach as seen below for identifying the guiding principles.

Identifying the steering convictions

Leadership chooses a real-life situation in the recent past in which the issue was rampant. From memory the leadership describes the situation as concrete and precise as possible, like a film with moving images. They characterize the described situation by formulating what was striking in the description. The leadership tries to identify a dominant principle as it appears in the behavior of the leadership acting in the situation. They analyze how things went in the process and whether there is an indication for the need of change of this guiding principle. What could be a new guiding principle, which might direct the behavior and acting of the leadership in a new way leading to targeted outcomes?

In this way, the leadership can gain insights into the dominant steering convictions that direct their actions and behavior in real situations. This can lead to impulses to search for new ideas, open up to new experiences in new unknown situations, and integrate these new experiences and insights into their acting and behavior.

We described three opportunities for the leadership to act, in which the leadership can consciously apply this horizontal leadership methodology, experience it and learn to see it. This raises the leadership's sensitivity while being involved in processes of organization development, change and innovation in social reality.

6. Using the horizontal leadership methodology

How can this methodology be applied as a horizontal leadership method-ology in processes of organization development?

I will describe the systematic application of the methodology of horizontal leadership in an organizational development process within the organized community.

The leader of the community rises to a question. The question has become evident in frictions, incidents, conflicts, breaking through patterns, processes of value creation or destruction. The question is verbalized in the context of the community involved. This creates the start of a process of development.

When the leader takes the responsibility to tackle the question, a process of change and innovation starts and organizational development and sensegiving emerge.

The question is researched by the leader. Who is connected to this question? Did we see this question arise before in the biography of this organized community? How is the question alive in the inner world of people involved? How long ago did we see this question come up and what do we expect for the future to appear?

In a circular process, the leader searches for people who can shed some more light on the question. Stories are written down, reflections and memories are being documented. Also, interpretations and judgments are being registered. As how serious, how existential did the people involved experience the question, what tension did it rise, what meaning did it trigger. The one responding points to the next one to be talked to by the leader, until there is no more new information coming to the surface.

The leader also searches for facts and data that can support or contradict the stories uncovered. By actual observations and analyzing material, the picture of the question gets more body. The person responsible experiences the question in practice and observes it, together with others. Through checking in an empirical way how the people involved have seen the question, it becomes clear that the question is relevant for the community and that it plays a role in the interaction and experience of people involved.

The person in charge reflects on the research, the interventions and how the question came alive and changed during the research process. Opportunities for change appear in the social reality. They become visible: changes in constellations of people, in work processes, in steering convictions are initiated.

Applying this horizontal leadership methodology makes the question become observable and the people in the process find opportunities to work together on that question. A process of consciousness building and decision making around this social question arises. The opportunities to take initiative open up.